QUILT PANEL MAGIC

15 Projects with a Creative Twist

CYNDI MCCHESNEY

C&T PUBLISHING
Another Maker Inspired!

Dedication

In loving memory of my mom,
Sylvia McChesney, my biggest cheerleader.

In my journey as a quiltmaker, author, and designer, I have been gifted with friendships and encouragement from a great many people. To my students who kept asking questions and pushing me to be a better teacher, thank you! To Alex Anderson and Ricky Tims for inviting me to appear as a guest on **TheQuiltShow.com**. This opened a door, allowing me to step into a world of creativity I didn't know existed within me—a **huge** thank you! To my closest friends and my aunts (you know who you are) who allowed me to vent, cry, share, and accept feedback. Without you, I wouldn't be where I am today: Thank you doesn't seem like enough, so let me also say I love and appreciate you! And finally, to the **amazing** team of contributors, Marie, Terry, Adam, Tonya, Heikei, Margaret, Jacki, Kathryn, Laura, and Susan, who helped show how these patterns could be adapted for other panels and tested instructions—you are the **best**!

Acknowledgments

The representatives from Benartex, QT Fabrics, Riley Blake Designs, Clothworks, Wilmington Prints, Timeless Treasures Fabrics, and Henry Glass Fabrics have been amazing to work with. Thank you for providing panels and coordinating fabrics for most of the projects in this book.

All the quilts in this book are designed, constructed, and quilted by me. I also quilted and bound all the contributor quilts. My go-to supplies include Synthrapol, Aurifil 50-weight two-ply thread for piecing, Quilters Dream Batting, and Signature 40-weight cotton thread for quilting.

CONTENTS

Projects for Solo Panels   17

Celebration **18**

A Bucketful of Sunshine **26**

Santa's Coming! **33**

Projects for Uniform-Size Multi-Image Panels   43

Besties **44**

Hip to Be Square **51**

When Night Falls, the Forest Sings **56**

Spooky Table Runner **66**

TRICK-OR-TREAT BAG **72**

Spooky Place Mats **74**

FESTIVE POT HOLDER **83**

Projects for Companion Image Panels 85

Winter Serenity **86**

Coffee, Tea, or Cocoa? **98**

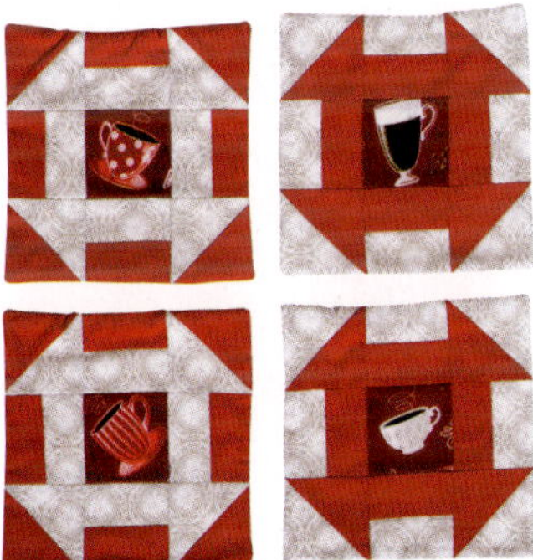

MUG MATS **104**

Cat Nap **106**

Large Tote Bag **118**

INTRODUCTION

When I completed my second book, *Playful Panel Quilts* (by C&T Publishing), I never imagined taking on a project of this magnitude! I had only recently dipped my toe into the world of producing patterns for others to replicate, and the idea of creating a dozen projects centered around panels seemed quite daunting—yet here we are!

I hope you will find a project or two that sparks your interest, and I wholeheartedly encourage you to explore how my team of contributors expressed themselves with different panels by using these patterns as springboards for their own creativity.

Panel enthusiasts will see that it is easy to insert most solo (single-image) panels into one of the three designs presented for that style panel by using a little math to adjust sizes to fit (a.k.a. coping strips!). Most solo panels are pretty close in size, so substituting colors and perhaps a block or two will allow you to personalize any of these designs.

If you are a lover of multi-image panels, the quilts presented in this category will also be fairly easy to customize because … you guessed it! Multi-image panels also come in similar sizes, and for some of the patterns, I've provided a chart for resizing the units if you choose a different size panel image! Be sure to check out the section on alternate blocks to use, because you could easily swap out a different block in some of the designs!

Although a little harder to find, panels with a single large and several smaller companion images can also be adapted. Take a look at how the contributors modified the patterns to create quilts to accommodate the panels they chose.

Just for fun, I've included a sampling of smaller projects, from home decor ideas to bags and more. These projects are quick and fun and a great solution for using up leftover panel images or coordinating fabrics from other projects.

Do take the time to read through the General Instructions (page 7). There is **a lot** of useful info there that will keep you from making mistakes in the patterns.

I'd love to see what you do with the project instructions, so please share photos with me at **cyndimcchesney@gmail.com** and/or sign up for my newsletter at **cedarridgequilting.com**

Create some fun, and happy sewing!

GENERAL INSTRUCTIONS

BEFORE YOU BEGIN

Many of the projects in this book use the construction techniques in this chapter. Take the time to read this chapter carefully before you begin. For common blocks and units, use your preferred construction method, but remember, it is essential that you confirm the **cut and/or finished size** of each unit to ensure success.

Choosing Panels and Fabrics

Although the panels featured in the projects may or may not be available, look for panels with a similar size and theme or follow the tips for using a different panel, including trimming, adding coping strips, or selecting different accompanying blocks.

Choose a palette of light, medium, and dark fabrics or try a scrappy mix for a fun and unique result. Including too many busy prints will muddy the design, so use caution when adding prints to the fabric palette. Solids, textured solids, or small prints work best to maintain the basic design and keep your panel the focal point of your quilt.

Panel Preparation

Panels come with their own set of challenges, from appearing wonky at the start to having odd measurements, and knowing what to do to fix these issues will help you achieve a successful project. These steps are absolutely crucial, so take the time to understand how to square your panels and adjust them to fit into the designated space. The projects have been designed with standard panel sizes to provide you with the versatility to use them with panels from your stash or newly available panels.

Start by washing the panel (this general rule goes for all panels, whether one or multiple images). I suggest using a delicate detergent, such as Synthrapol, because it won't strip out the color and will remove excess dye. I wash on the delicate cycle in cold water and only dry my panels for about fifteen minutes so that they are still slightly damp when they come out of the dryer. This allows me to square up my panels before I begin working; see Squaring Up Panel Images (page 7).

CUTTING APART MULTI-IMAGE PANELS

Determining what you want to keep or what can be trimmed away when using multi-image panels is a personal preference. The projects in this book use specific-size panel images, but the contributors who made quilts from the project instructions were often working with panel images of different sizes and made simple adjustments to accommodate them.

Before you decide whether you can simply trim the panel images, add coping strips, or tackle the math of adjusting the instructions, cut the images apart as follows.

Some panel images are printed in a manner that has each image touching the next image. In this instance, identify the line separating the two images and cut on that line, *even if it is not straight!* You will straighten them up after they have been cut apart.

If there is background fabric between the panel images, measure the space between the images and cut them apart equidistant from one another. In other words, if there is a 1˝ space between images, cut ½˝ around each image. This margin usually ends up being trimmed away or becomes part of the seam allowance.

SQUARING UP PANEL IMAGES

Be sure that all panel images are square before trimming, adding coping strips, or using them in a patchwork block!

Solo Panels

My first step is to determine whether there is something I can use as a reference for a clean-cut edge. Perhaps the panel has a printed border or, at the very least, a space of solid background fabric to use as a reference.

I make a clean cut at a set measurement along the outside of the printed border to ensure that the panel is cut accurately. Be sure to add the seam allowance before you cut!

Next, fold the top to the bottom, aligning the selvedges, and check that the panel is laying flat and the sides are lined up.

It can be tricky to square up large solo panels, so try blocking them. After prewashing, but before it is fully dry, I pin the panel to my design wall. To prepare my design wall, I add a blocking sheet created from large sheets of stabilizer. I draw lines at 90° angles on the sheets to provide reference points. Pin the panel to the blocking sheet, placing pins every 2˝–3˝. Allow the panel to dry in place and then lightly starch and press with a lift-and-set motion of the iron. Don't move the iron back and forth across the fabric, as this method can cause stretching and distortion.

Blocking a full panel

Multi-Image Panels

Before I attempt to square up the individual images in a multi-image panel, I cut them apart; see Cutting Apart Multi-Image Panels (page 7).

To square up a panel image, select any logical line of the image—I generally choose the top.

1. Align a ruler edge along that line to determine how not square the piece is. This step will show you which sides or corners you'll need to manipulate to straighten the image. *fig. A*

2. With a spray bottle of water, lightly mist the fabric. Iron the corner or section of the image until it is as square as possible. Work slowly and check the shape regularly. *fig. B*

3. Spritz, press, check with the ruler, and repeat until the image is as straight as you can manage. *fig. C*

4. Finally, spray it lightly with starch, place something flat (such as a large ruler) over the piece, and stack some books on top until it has dried into the shape you want to achieve.

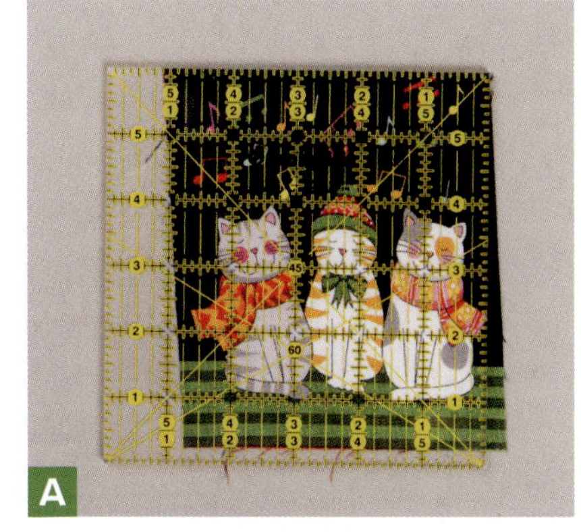

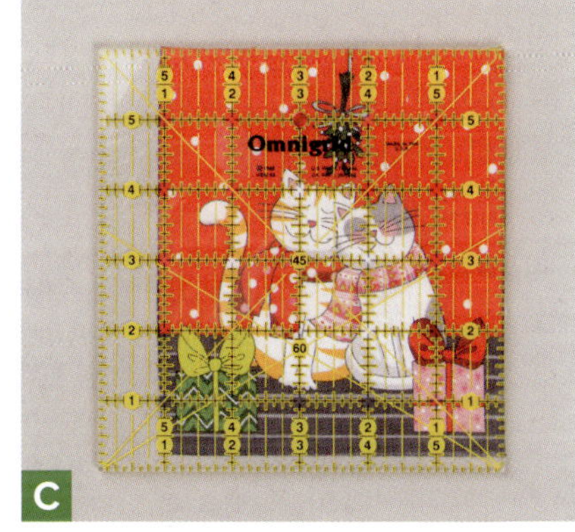

TRIMMING PANEL IMAGES

Smaller panels allow you to identify the center of the frame or design and use it as a reference point when trimming. Occasionally, you can simply trim ¼˝ around the frame of the image, but generally, you'll need to locate the center and measure equally from that point.

COPING STRIPS

Whether you are working with a large solo panel or smaller images from a multi-image panel, coping strips are useful when a panel segment is too small for the space allowed. To bring it up to the size needed, you may have to add strips to some or all of the edges of the image. Coping strips are not the same as a border because they serve the purpose of getting you from the size you have to the size you need.

TIP

Square up first! Before you do anything to the panel images—trimming them or adding coping strips—be sure to square them up!

For example, let's say your panel image finishes at 4½˝, but it needs to finish at 6˝ to fit the space in the design.

Knowing that your image has to be 6˝, determine the difference between where you're going (6˝) and where you are (4½˝). The difference is 1½˝. I prefer to keep the coping strips the same size whenever possible, but it's not a requirement. What is important is that the math works!

Divide 1½˝ by 2 to make the strips the same size on each edge (in this case, ¾˝ for each edge). Cut the strips 1¼˝ wide to include the ¼˝ seam allowance on both sides of the strip.

Let's walk through this process in detail:

If you are working with square panels, as in this example, you will be adding coping strips of the same width to all sides. But if you are working with rectangles, the width might vary between the top and bottom strips and the side strips. Just work through the process separately for each pair.

Decide if you are adding the top and bottom strips first or the sides. We will add the sides first.

1. Calculate the difference between the needed finished image (6″ × 6″) and your panel (4½″ × 4½″), then divide by 2 to determine the finished width of each coping strip.

 6″ – 4½″ = 1½″

 1½″ / 2 = ¾″ finished coping strip width

Add ½″ to the finished coping strip to account for seam allowances on each side.

 ¾″ × ½″ = 1¼″ unfinished coping strip width

2. The panel image finishes at 4½″ × 4½″, so cut it at 5″ × 5″ to include seam allowances.

3. Cut 2 strips the unfinished coping strip width × the unfinished panel width (1¼″ × 5″) and add them to the sides of the panel.

4. The top and bottom coping strips are cut the unfinished coping strip width × the unfinished width of the panel, (1¼″ × 6½″). This accounts for the width you have now added to the sides of the image.

5. The panel piece should now measure 6½″ × 6½″, which will finish at 6″ × 6″.

For your reference, and to make working with coping strips as simple as possible, I am including a copy of the Coping Strip Calculator Worksheet originally created by Sophie Scardaci of C&T Publishing. You may copy the worksheet for your personal use only. This worksheet takes you through every step needed to do the math to produce successful coping strips!

Coping Strip Calculator

When using the calculator, remember:

- Do not trim or cut coping until math is complete.

- Finished Size does not include seam allowance.

- All measurements are in inches.

- **Note:** Do not just add a long coping strip and cut it off at the bottom—this will result in stretching and distortion.

Enter the following dimensions:					
Goal Size of Panel (Finished Dimensions):	Width		Height		
Starting Size of Panel (Finished Dimensions)	Width		Height		
CUT MEASUREMENTS					
Trim Panel (Finished Size plus seam allowance)	Width		Height		
If adding Coping Strips to the Top/Bottom of panel before Vertical Sides:					
Cut 2 for Top/Bottom	Width		Length		
Cut 2 for Sides	Width		Length		
If adding Coping Strips to the Vertical Sides of panel before Top/Bottom:					
Cut 2 for Top/Bottom	Width		Length		
Cut 2 for Sides	Width		Length		

Borders and blocks can be revised and replaced to adjust the level of complexity or to match a differently themed panel.

Adjust the project to your desired level of complexity by using a simpler or more intricate block in place of the indicated block. For example, a Sparkling Star block could be replaced with a simple Flying Geese unit, or a simple Four-Patch could be replaced by a Pinwheel. What is most important is that the new unit must be the same finished size for the quilt design to work!

If you select a panel with a different theme than the project panel, you could swap out appliqué blocks, change colors, switch a patchwork element, or simply turn an element, such as a Dresden Plate, upside down to look more like a wreath than patriotic bunting! For example, if the project panel features a Christmas theme and you choose a completely different panel, you may opt to swap a Candy Cane block for something more appropriate. The contributor's quilts, which follow each project, offer great examples of exactly this idea.

Your imagination will help you create a unique variation of your own!

FUNDAMENTALS

Basic Patchwork Units

In the following pages, I'm presenting the most beginner-friendly method for constructing each of the units shown. There is always more than one way to make a block, so let your experience guide you.

There are specialty rulers and numerous other construction techniques that you may prefer or be more familiar or comfortable with. Use what works for you—just be sure that the cut and finished size of the unit is what is called for in the project!

My personal preference is to make most units oversize and then trim to the cut size needed for the project to ensure accurate patchwork. If you choose a different patchwork technique, just be sure that the

result is the one you want! It's always a good idea to make a test block using some scrap fabric.

PRESSING YOUR UNITS

I generally press almost all of my seam allowances open. I hear your gasp! I do this step to reduce bulk throughout my project.

I also tighten up my stitch length, generally sewing with a stitch length of 2.0. If you're not concerned about bulk, then by all means press to one side, but try to nest your seam allowances (pressing them in opposite directions from one another where they meet) whenever possible. Pressing instructions in the projects are suggestions but might yield the best results if followed.

Press the pieced patchwork with a dry iron. Steam tends to distort your patchwork and your panel pieces once you have taken the time to square them. If you absolutely must steam your patchwork, mist with a spray bottle of water as needed and a starch product if you like. Use a **light** touch with the iron; this is not the place for muscle. An up-and-down motion instead of a side-to-side motion will yield more accurate results.

HALF-SQUARE TRIANGLES (HSTS)

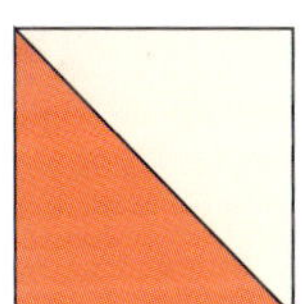

1. Pair 2 squares right sides together.

2. Draw a diagonal line from one corner to the opposite corner on the wrong side of the lighter fabric.

3. Stitch a scant ¼˝ seam along each side of the drawn line.
fig. A

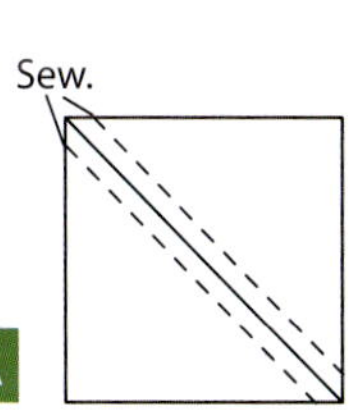

4. Cut apart the 2 triangles on the drawn line and press, either to one side or open.

5. Trim each HST to the size noted in the project instructions. For example, if the HST should finish at 2˝ × 2˝, trim to 2½˝ × 2½˝. Notice that the diagonal line of the ruler should be lined up on the seam. For the first trim, center the ruler over the oversize unit and trim 2 sides (right and top for right-handed quilters, left and top for left-handed quilters). Rotate the unit 180° and align the diagonal ruler line with the seam and the 2 trimmed edges with the cut size of the unit. Trim the remaining side and top. *fig. B*

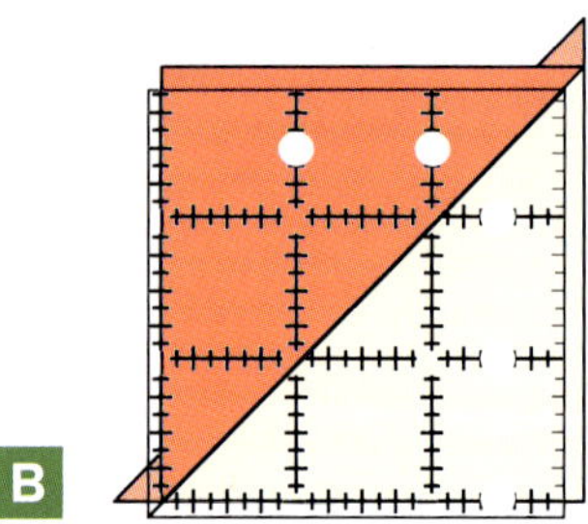 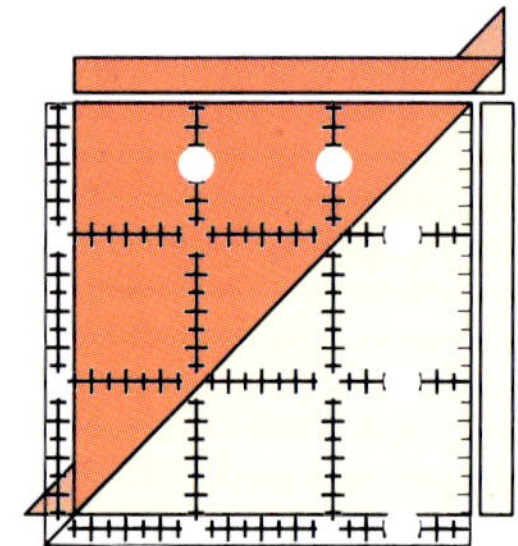 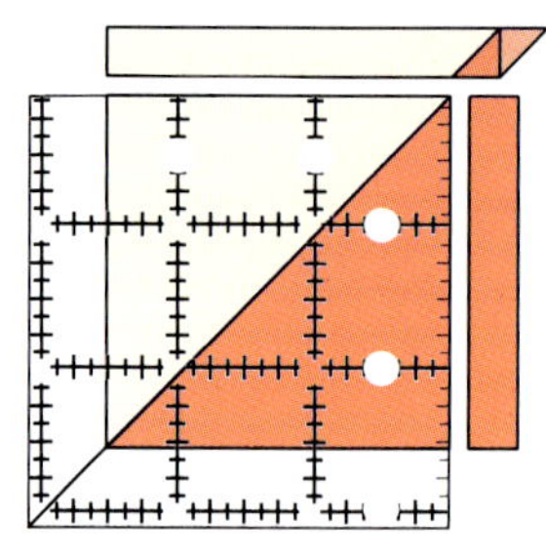 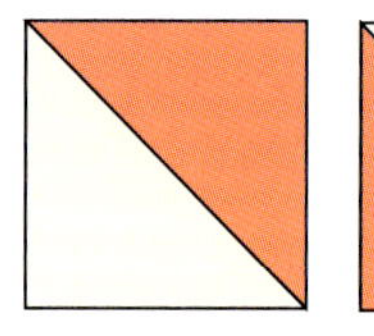 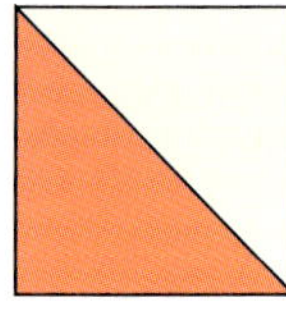

B

COMBINATION TRIANGLE UNITS

1. Follow Steps 1–3 for Half-Square Triangles (HSTs) (page 11).

2. Cut apart the 2 triangles on the drawn line and press, either to one side or open. **Do not trim** yet!

3. Pair each HST with another square, right sides together. *fig. C*

4. Draw a diagonal line from one corner to the opposite corner on the wrong side of the HST.

C

5. Stitch a scant ¼˝ along each side of the drawn line.

6. Cut apart the 2 triangles on the drawn line and press. *fig. D*

7. Trim, lining up the diagonal line of the ruler with the long diagonal seam and with the center point of the cut size of the unit positioned at the intersection of the long and short diagonal lines. For example, if the unit is to be trimmed to 4½˝, place the 2¼˝ point of the square on the intersection of those 2 seams.

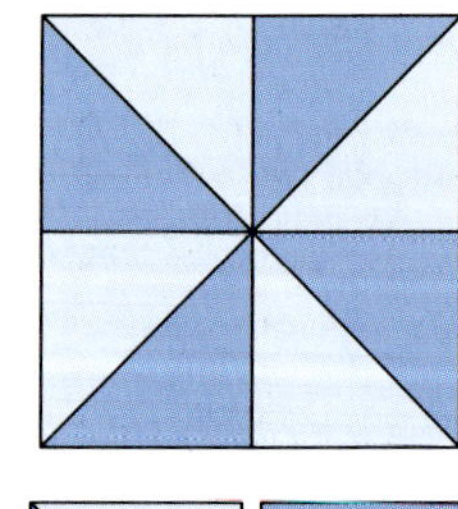

D

8. Rotate the unit 180° and line the diagonal with the seam and the 2 trimmed edges with the cut size of the unit. Trim the remaining side and top. *fig. E*

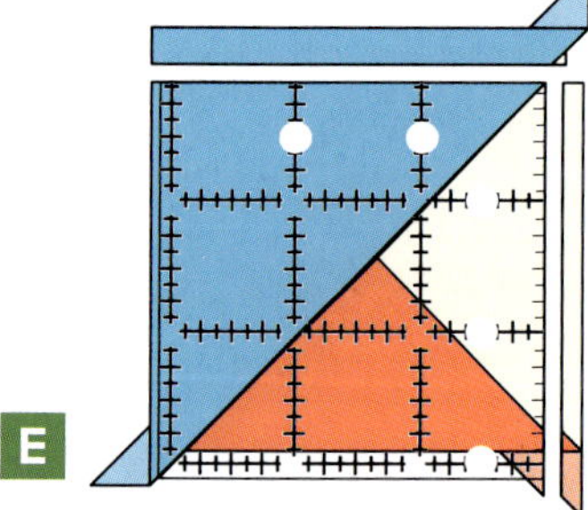 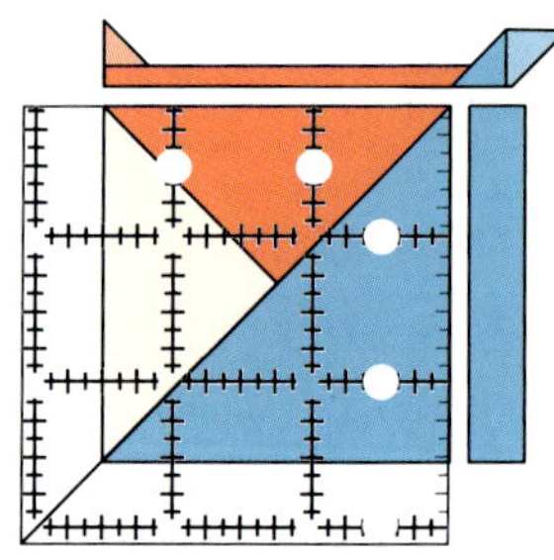

E

PINWHEELS

Pinwheels are created from four Half-Square Triangles (HSTs) (page 11). The trick is in the layout. Refer to the diagram for how to lay out the unit and piece it together. *fig. F*

F

FLYING GEESE (FG)

You will need 1 rectangle and 2 squares to construct FG with this method.

1. Draw a diagonal line from one corner to the opposite corner on the wrong side of each of the 2 squares.

2. Place 1 square on the rectangle, right sides together and lined up at one end, with the drawn

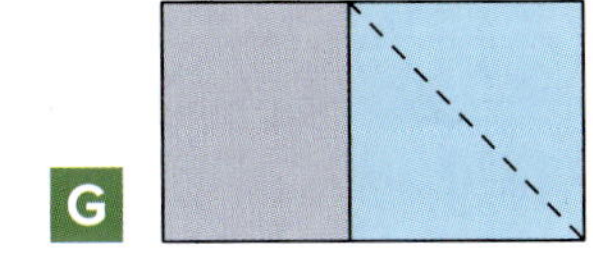

line pointing toward the center of the rectangle. *fig. G*

3. Stitch along the drawn line.

4. Trim ¼˝ from the sewn line and press away from the rectangle (toward the triangle piece).

5. Layer the second square, right sides together, on the other end of the rectangle, with the drawn

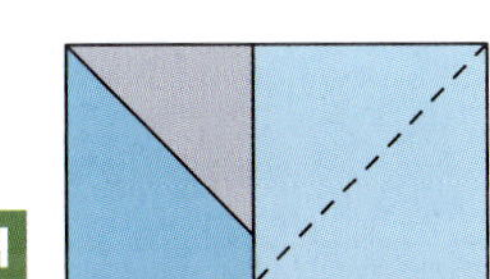

line pointing toward the center. Stitch along the diagonal drawn line. *fig. H*

6. Trim ¼˝ from the sewn line and press away from the center (toward the

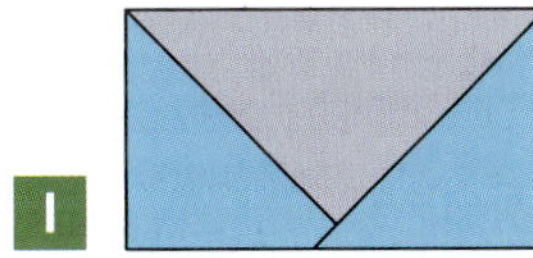

triangle piece). *fig. I*

SNOWBALL CORNERS

Snowball Corners can be created with 1 or more small corner squares by using this simple stitch-and-flip method.

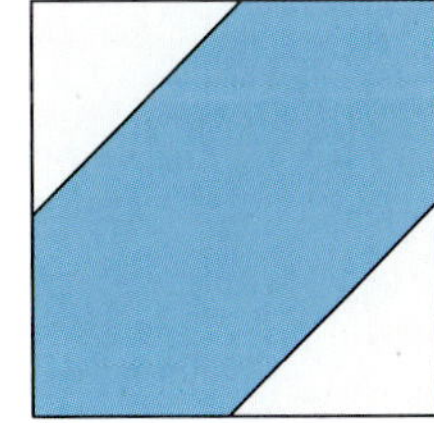

1. Draw a diagonal line from one corner to the opposite corner on the wrong side of the smaller square(s).

2. Place a smaller square in 1 corner of the larger square, right sides together. Be sure that the drawn line is oriented to touch 2 outside edges of the large square.

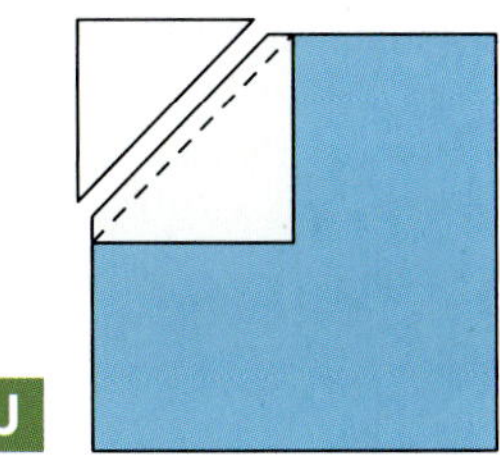

3. Stitch along the line. *fig. J*

4. Trim away the excess from the outside of the corner and press the smaller square away from the center of the large square.

STRIP SETS

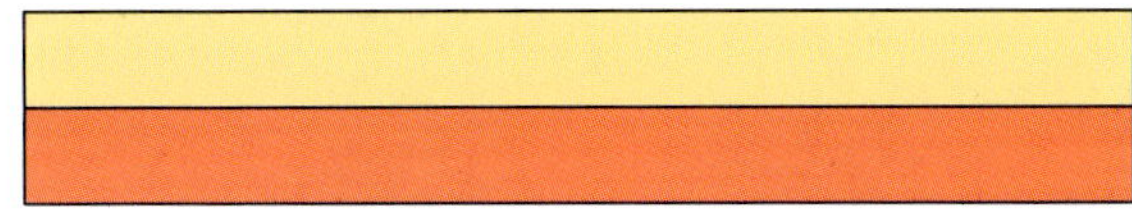

1. Cut strips at the size indicated in the project instructions across the width of fabric (WOF).

2. Sew strips right sides together along the long edge as shown. In **most** instances, the subcut sets are the same width as the original cut size of the strip. For example, if you cut your strips 2˝ × WOF and sew 2 strips together, you would subcut units every 2˝ apart to produce a unit that is 2˝ × 3½˝. If you are sewing 3 or more strips together, you would **still** subcut every 2˝! *fig. K*

DRESDEN PLATES

Although I prefer to use a Dresden Plate blade template, such as the EZ Quilting Easy Dresden Ruler by Darlene Zimmerman, when creating my units for a Dresden Plate, I've provided a Dresden Plate blade template (page 121). Cut templates from freezer paper, template plastic, or Mylar.

1. Cut a strip of fabric the same width as the length of the blade. Cut the required number of blades.

2. Fold each blade in half, right sides together, and stitch ¼˝ along the top edge.

3. Trim away a small triangle off the corner near the folded edge. *fig. L*

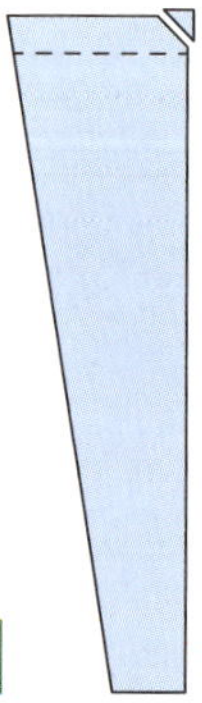

4. Turn the point and gently push the corner out, making sure that the point is in line with the center fold of the blade, and press. *fig. M*

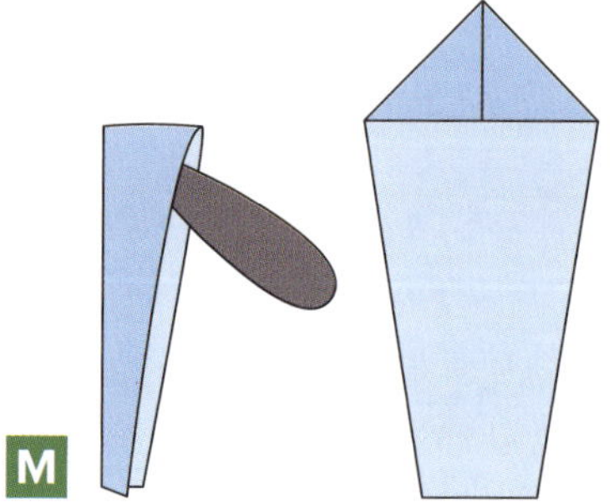

5. When stitching the blades together, be sure to backstitch at the folded edge.

Use the Circle template (page 122) to appliqué the center of your Dresden Plate. The circle can be cut in half or quarters to suit the units called for in the individual projects.

Adjusting Block Sizes

When using a small panel image within a block or when selecting a panel that is a different size from the one indicated in the project, you have options.

If your image is larger, consider trimming to size; see Trimming Panel Images (page 9). If your image is smaller, you could add coping strips; see Coping Strips (page 9). You could also adjust the block within which the panel is featured to the size needed for your panel image.

The first two options are the easiest, but if you believe your math skills are up to the challenge, changing the size of the blocks (and, thus, the size of the entire quilt) is definitely an option.

See how two contributors did this with their quilts. Jump to Kathryn Oliphant's *Guitar Passion* (page 55) and Heikei Kovacich's *Liam's Quilt* (page 103). For an in-depth primer on how to adjust block sizes, dive into my first two books, *Fun with Panels* and *Playful Panel Quilts*, both by C&T Publishing.

Machine Appliqué

Included on pages 121–125 are the appliqué templates for the projects in this book as well as a couple of extras to swap if you'd like.

I use a raw-edge fusible appliqué method with a blanket stitch done by machine. As with many other techniques in quiltmaking, there is more than one way to appliqué a star! Choose the method that best meets your abilities and your personality.

SWAPPING BLOCKS TO MATCH YOUR PANEL

When selecting the blocks to use in the projects in this book, I looked for quilt blocks that already had big open spaces, such as a Sawtooth Star (see below) or a block where I could leave an element or a section out to create space, such as the Dutch Rose, featured in the quilt *When Night Falls, the Forest Sings* (page 56).

Here are some additional blocks that could work in the same way; just double-check that the math works out!

The blocks below come from *The New Quick & Easy Block Tool* and *The New Ladies' Art Company Quick and Easy Block Tool*, both by C&T Publishing.

Alternate Blocks for 6″ × 6″ Finished-Size Panel Images

By leaving out the 6″ × 6″ center of each of these 12″ × 12″ pieced blocks, you can create a space in which to insert a 6″ × 6″ panel image. Play around and have fun!

Sawtooth Star

Storm at Sea

Homegrown

Ocean Waves

Sparkling Star

Balkan Puzzle

Constellation

Windmill

Alternate Blocks for 8″ × 8″ Finished-Size Panel Images

By leaving out the 8″ × 8″ center of each of these 12″ × 12″ pieced blocks, you can create a space in which to insert an 8″ × 8″ panel image.

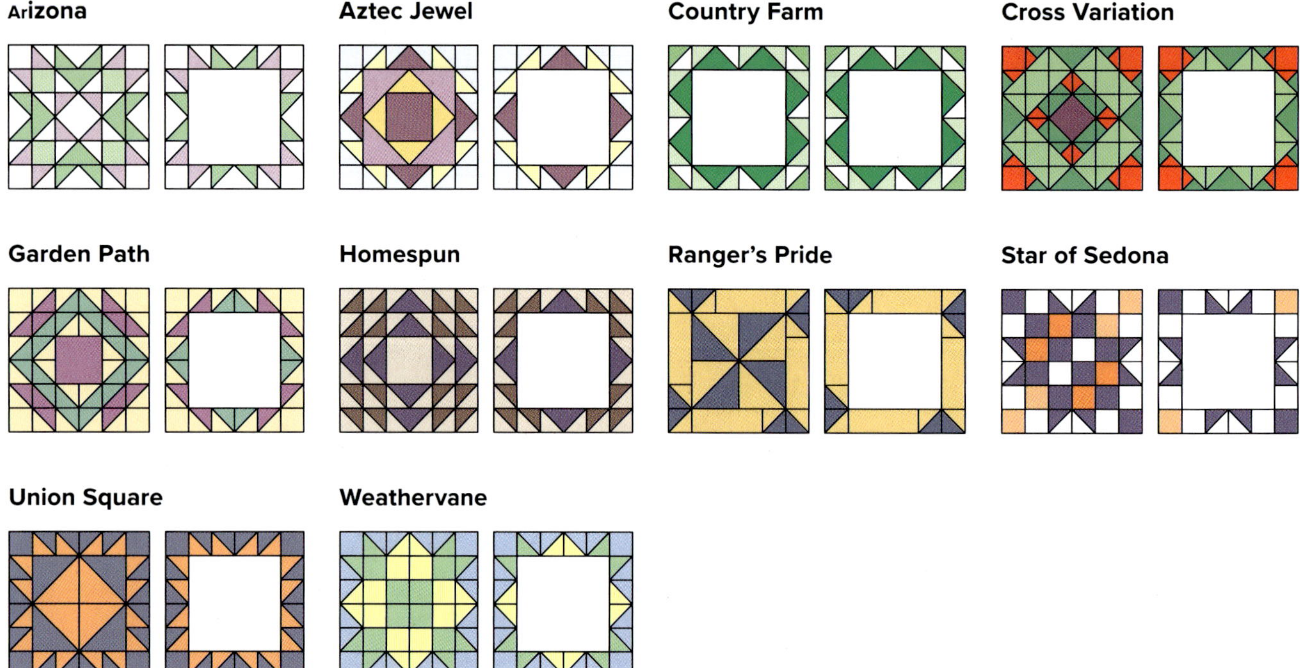

FINISHING

After quilting my quilts, I generally use a double-fold straight-grain binding. I like to find interesting prints or stripes to use in the binding for an extra surprise, but binding is, like all choices in making a quilt, personal. If you prefer to make the binding the same color or many colors, or if you choose to use a facing in place of a binding, **do it**!

Add a label to your quilt citing the pattern name and designer, your name, the quilter's name, the date you completed your quilt, and the location. Documenting is an important part of making a quilt. You can create your own labels by using photo-transfer fabric or by simply pressing some white fabric to a sheet of freezer paper and writing on it with an archival pen or running it through your printer.

PROJECTS FOR SOLO PANELS

Each of the projects in this chapter features a solo panel. In general, solo panel images can be found in two sizes: approximately 22˝–24˝ × 40˝–42˝ and approximately 36˝ × 42˝.

I have created two projects for the more popular panel size of 22˝–24˝ × 40˝–42˝. Each project includes instructions on how to accommodate any similar-size panel. The contributor quilts demonstrate how to take each pattern and customize it for a different season, holiday, or motif.

The larger panels are featured less frequently; thus, I have designed only one project for this size. You will see from my and the contributor's quilt that it can easily accommodate slight differences in size and be customized to reflect the theme of the panel you choose.

Have fun!

Celebration

Design Suggestions

Although I designed this quilt with a patriotic theme, several of the components could be rotated to showcase another theme and panel, such as *Merry Snowmen* by Jacki Montplaisar (page 25). Take a look at what Jacki did to create a wintry feel.

Celebrate the red, white, and blue for the Fourth of July, Memorial Day, or a special veteran in your life. This quilt features the Stars & Stripes *panel by Timeless Treasures, but any single-image panel that fits the theme can be adapted to work in this design. In addition to the panel, I used several Timeless Treasures and other fabrics that coordinated with the color palette.*

Materials

Yardages are based on 41˝-wide fabric.

Panel: Single-image panel approximately 24˝ × 42˝. I used *Stars & Stripes* by Timeless Treasures.

White: 2⅛ yards

Navy blue: 1⅜ yards

Medium blue: ⅔ yard

Medium-light blue: ½ yard

Dark red: ⅞ yard

Red: ⅞ yard

Red and white stripe: ¾ yard (for binding and border spacers)

Backing: 3¼ yards

Batting: 60˝ × 78˝

Flag templates (page 121)

Dresden Plate blade template (page 121) or EZ Quilting Easy Dresden Ruler by Darlene Zimmerman

Circle template (page 122)

Cutting

All pieces for patchwork and appliqué elements in this quilt are subcut from the following strips.

White

Cut 3 strips 6½˝ × WOF (width of fabric).

Cut 2 strips 5½˝ × WOF.

Cut 8 strips 3˝ × WOF.

Cut 1 strip 2½˝ × WOF.

Cut 3 strips 2˝ × WOF.

Cut 4 strips 1½˝ × WOF.

Navy Blue

Cut 1 strip 6½˝ × WOF.

Cut 1 strip 5½˝ × WOF.

Cut 1 strip 4½˝ × WOF.

Cut 3 strips 3˝ × WOF.

Cut 6 strips 2½˝ × WOF.

Medium Blue

Cut 1 strip 5½˝ × WOF.

Cut 1 strip 4½˝ × WOF.

Cut 2 strips 3˝ × WOF.

Cut 1 strip 2˝ × WOF.

Medium-Light Blue

Cut 1 strip 4½˝ × WOF.

Cut 2 strips 3˝ × WOF.

Cut 1 strip 2˝ × WOF.

Dark Red

Cut 1 strip 4½˝ × WOF.

Cut 3 strips 3˝ × WOF.

Cut 5 strips 2½˝ × WOF.

Red

Cut 2 strips 5½˝ × WOF.

Cut 1 strip 4½˝ × WOF.

Cut 1 strip 3½˝ × WOF.

Cut 1 strip 3˝ × WOF.

Red and White Stripe

Cut 1 strip 6½˝ × WOF.

Cut 7 strips 2½˝ × WOF.

CONSTRUCTION

Before beginning any project, read the General Instructions (page 7). This project uses construction techniques for Half-Square Triangles (HSTs) (page 11), Combination Triangle units (page 12), and Flying Geese units (page 13).

Panel Preparation

Adjust your panel to 22½˝ × 40½˝. Be sure that the panel is squared up! See Squaring Up Panel Images (page 7).

CUTTING

Cut 2 white coping strips 1½˝ × 40½˝.

Cut 2 white coping strips 1½˝ × 24½˝.

ASSEMBLY

Press all seam allowances open unless otherwise noted.

1. Sew the white strips 1½˝ × 40½˝ to the left and right sides of the panel.

2. Sew the white strips 1½˝ × 24½˝ to the top and bottom of the panel.

Friendship Star Blocks

FINISHED BLOCK: 6˝ × 6˝

Make 4.

CUTTING

Cut 8 red squares 3˝ × 3˝.

Cut 8 white squares 3˝ × 3˝.

Cut 16 white squares 2½˝ × 2½˝.

Cut 4 navy blue squares 2½˝ × 2½˝.

ASSEMBLY

Press all seam allowances open unless otherwise noted.

1. Pair a red square 3˝ × 3˝ and a white square 3˝ × 3˝ to make 2 HSTs. Repeat to make 4 HSTs per block (16 total). Press and trim to 2½˝ × 2½˝.

2. Using 4 white squares 2½˝ × 2½˝ for the corners, 4 HSTs, and 1 navy blue square 2½˝ × 2½˝ for the center, lay out the block as illustrated. *fig. A*

3. Stitch each row as shown. Press the seam allowances toward the squares. *fig. B*

4. Sew the 3 rows together and press.

Sawtooth Star Blocks

FINISHED BLOCK: 6˝ × 6˝

Make 4.

CUTTING

Cut 4 red squares 3½˝ × 3½˝.

Cut 16 white squares 2˝ × 2˝.

Cut 16 white rectangles 2˝ × 3½˝.

Cut 16 medium-light blue squares 2˝ × 2˝.

Cut 16 medium blue squares 2˝ × 2˝.

ASSEMBLY

Press all seam allowances open unless otherwise noted.

1. Using 1 white rectangle 2˝ × 3½˝, 1 medium-light blue square 2˝ × 2˝ on the right end of the rectangle, and 1 medium blue square 2˝ × 2˝ on the left end of the rectangle, make an FG unit (page 13). Make 16 FG units.

2. Refer to the Sawtooth Star block diagram and construct 4 blocks, using the red square 3½˝ × 3½˝ in the center of the block and 4 white squares 2˝ × 2˝ in the corners of the block with the FG units. Press. *fig. C*

Dresden Plate Blocks

Make 5 half- and 2 quarter-Dresden Plates.

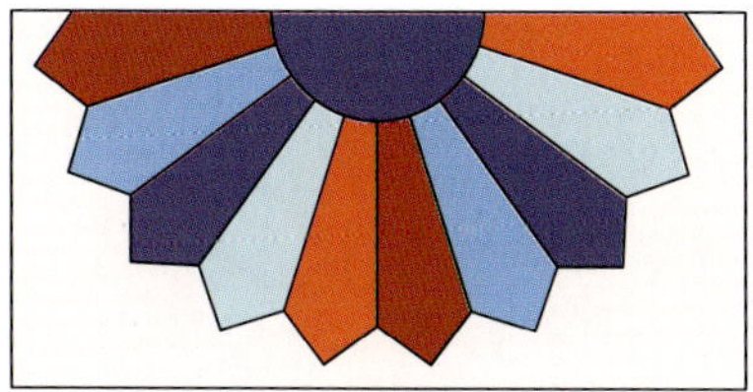

✂ CUTTING

From the 4½˝ × WOF strips of the red, dark red, navy blue, medium blue, and medium-light blue fabrics, subcut 12 blades of each color by using the Dresden Plate blade template (page 121) or ruler.

Cut 5 white rectangles 6½˝ × 12½˝.

Cut 2 white squares 6½˝ × 6½˝.

Using the Circle template (page 122), cut 3 navy blue circles. Subcut the circles in half and subcut 1 half-circle into quarters. *Optional:* Apply fusible stabilizer to the wrong side of the fabric before you cut out the circles.

ASSEMBLY

Press all seam allowances open unless otherwise noted.

1. Refer to the instructions for sewing Dresden Plates (page 14).

2. Stitch 10 blades together to form a half-Dresden Plate, being sure to backstitch at the pointed ends of the blades. Make 5.

3. Stitch 5 blades together to form the quarter-Dresden Plate, being sure to backstitch at the pointed ends of the blades. Make 2.

4. Mark the center of each 6½˝ × 12½˝ white rectangle. Align each half-plate with the center mark and pin securely.

5. Sew the half-plates to the white rectangles, ⅛˝ from the raw edge, and appliqué the blades in place.

6. Align the quarter-plates on 2 sides of the 6½˝ × 6½˝ white squares, ⅛˝ from the raw edge, and appliqué the blades in place.

7. Appliqué 3 navy blue half-circles to the half-Dresden Plate blocks and appliqué 2 navy blue quarter-circles to the quarter-Dresden Plate blocks.

Circle-Bunting Border

Sew the 3 half-Dresden Plate blocks together to form the top border. Set aside.

Flag-Bunting Border

✂ CUTTING

Cut 3 navy blue and 3 red striped flags by using the Flag template (page 121).

Cut 6 left and 6 right white triangles by using the Flag Background triangle template (page 121).

ASSEMBLY

Press all seam allowances open unless otherwise noted.

1. Mark the registration points from the Flag Background triangle and Flag templates onto the wrong side of the flags and the white triangles.

2. Match the registration points of a left white triangle with a flag and pin together. Sew and press the seam allowance toward the white triangle. Make 6.

3. Repeat Step 2 with the right white triangle.

4. Sew the 6 flags together, alternating navy blue with striped flags. Set aside.

Right-Side Inner-Border Assembly

1. Arrange the blocks as shown.

2. Sew the blocks together and press.

3. Sew this border to the right side of the panel. Press the seam allowance toward the panel.

Left-Side Inner-Border Assembly

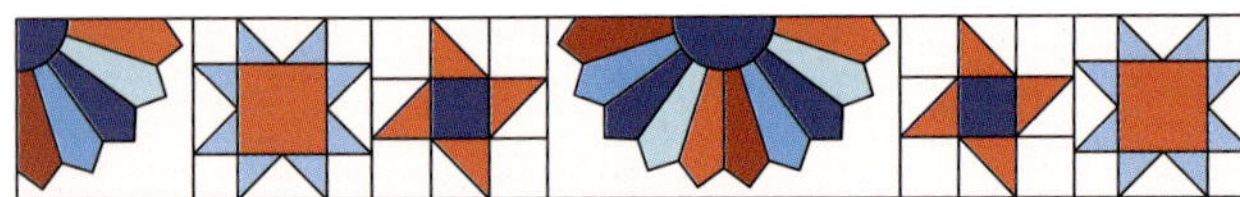

1. Arrange the blocks as shown.

2. Sew the blocks together and press.

3. Sew this border to the left side of the panel. Press the seam allowance toward the panel.

Add the Top and Bottom Inner Borders

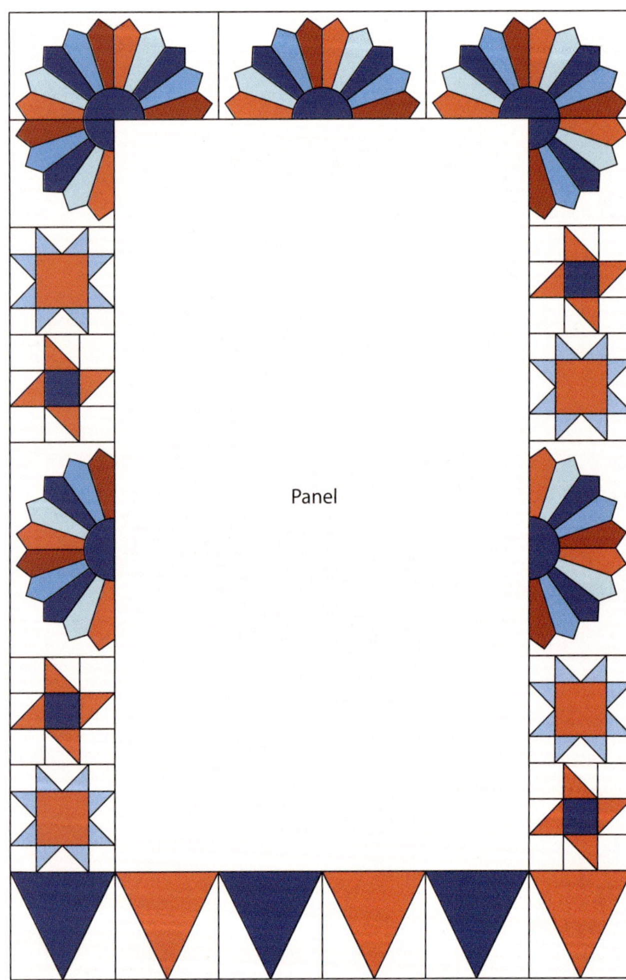

1. Sew the Circle-Bunting border to the top of the central panel.

2. Sew the Flag-Bunting border to the bottom of the central panel.

Outer-Pinwheel Border

CUTTING

Cut 28 navy blue squares 3˝ × 3˝.

Cut 2 navy blue strips 2½˝ × 36½˝.

Cut 1 navy blue strip 2½˝ × WOF in half to create 2 strips 2½˝ × 21˝.

Cut 14 medium blue squares 3˝ × 3˝.

Cut 14 medium-light blue squares 3˝ × 3˝.

Cut 32 dark red squares 3˝ × 3˝.

Cut 2 dark red strips 2½˝ × 36½˝.

Cut 1 dark red strip 2½˝ × WOF in half to create 2 strips 2½˝ × 21˝.

Cut 88 white squares 3˝ × 3˝.

Cut 2 red and white stripe rectangles 2½˝ × 4½˝.

ASSEMBLY

Press all seam allowances open unless otherwise noted.

1. Pair a 3˝ × 3˝ white square with a 3˝ × 3˝ navy blue square to make 2 HSTs. Repeat to make 56 dark blue and white HSTs. Press and trim to 2½˝ × 2½˝.

2. Repeat Step 1 to make 28 medium blue HSTs, 28 medium-light blue HSTs, and 64 dark red HSTs.

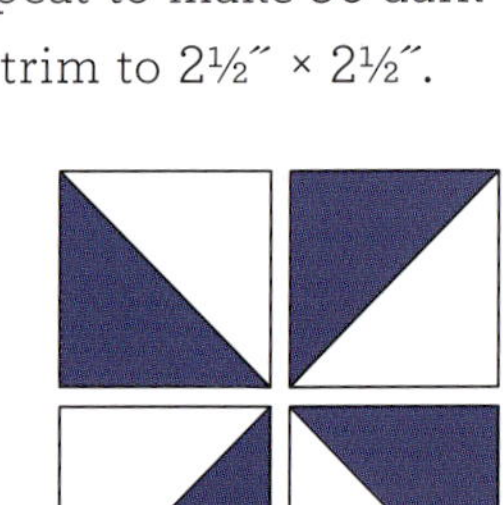

3. Arrange 4 navy blue/white HSTs to make a pinwheel block. *fig. D*

4. Sew each pair of HSTs together and press the seams in the opposite direction from one another. Sew the rows together and press.

5. Repeat Steps 3–4 to make 14 navy blue, 7 medium blue, 7 medium-light blue, and 16 red pinwheels 4½˝ × 4½˝.

6. Sew a navy blue strip 2½˝ × 21˝ to a navy blue strip 2½˝ × WOF. Make 2.

7. Trim each navy blue strip to 2½˝ × 54½˝.

8. Repeat Step 6 with a dark red strip 2½˝ × 21˝ and a dark red strip 2½˝ × WOF. Make 2. Trim to 2½˝ × 54½˝.

9. Arrange 9 pinwheels, a dark red strip 2½˝ × 36½˝, and a navy blue strip 2½˝ × 36½˝ as shown. *fig. E*

E

10. Sew the pinwheels together and press. Add the dark red and navy blue strips to either side and press. Make 2 units as shown.

11. Arrange 13 pinwheels, a red and white stripe spacer rectangle 2½˝ × 4½˝, a dark red strip 2½˝ × 54½˝, and a navy blue strip 2½˝ × 54½˝ as shown. *fig. F*

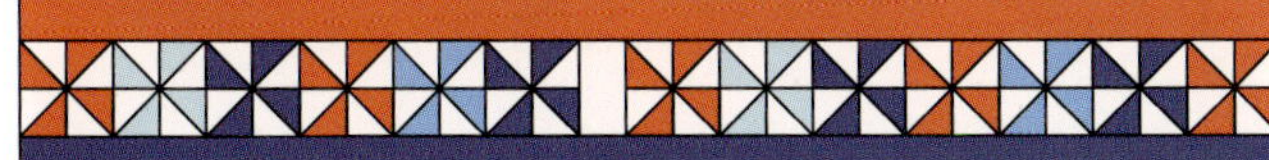

F

12. Sew the pinwheels and spacer rectangle together and press. Add the dark red and navy blue strips to either side and press. Make 2 units as shown.

Double-Pinwheel Corners

FINISHED BLOCK: 8˝ × 8˝

Construction will result in 4 units from each corner block that do not match the diagram. I discard these, but you may wish to save them for another project, such as a wall hanging or a pillow sham to coordinate with your quilt, or incorporate them into your backing.

CUTTING

Cut 12 red squares 5½˝ × 5½˝.

Cut 8 white squares 5½˝ × 5½˝.

Cut 6 navy blue squares 5½˝ × 5½˝.

Cut 6 medium blue squares 5½˝ × 5½˝.

DOUBLE-PINWHEEL 1 ASSEMBLY

1. Pair a white square 5½˝ × 5½˝ with a red square 5½˝ × 5½˝ to make 2 HSTs. Cut apart and press, but do not trim. Make 4 HSTs.

2. Pair each red/white HST with a navy blue square 5½˝ × 5½˝ and stitch. Cut apart and press. *fig. G*

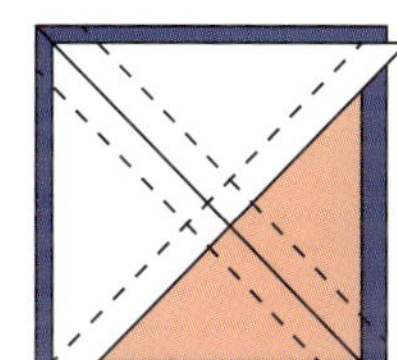

G

3. Trim 4 of the same units to 4½˝ × 4½˝. Discard the other four units.

4. Piece together 2 units for each row in the block. Piece the 2 rows together.

TIP

Be sure to check the general instructions for Half-Square Triangles (HSTs) (page 11) for how to trim these units correctly!

DOUBLE-PINWHEEL 2 ASSEMBLY

Repeat Steps 1–4 of the Double-Pinwheel 1 Assembly (above) with a white square 5½˝ × 5½˝ and a navy blue square 5½˝ × 5½˝ and a red square 5½˝ × 5½˝ for Step 2.

DOUBLE-PINWHEEL 3 ASSEMBLY

Repeat Steps 1–4 of the Double-Pinwheel 1 Assembly (page 23) with a white square 5½˝ × 5½˝ and a medium blue square 5½˝ × 5½˝ and a red square 5½˝ × 5½˝ for Step 2.

DOUBLE-PINWHEEL 4 ASSEMBLY

Repeat Steps 1–4 of the Double-Pinwheel 1 Assembly with a white square 5½˝ × 5½˝ and a red square 5½˝ × 5½˝ and a medium-blue square 5½˝ × 5½˝ for Step 2.

Outer-Border Assembly

1. Sew the longer pinwheel borders to the left and right sides of the quilt, with the dark red border toward the center of the quilt. Press the seam allowance toward the navy blue border.

2. Add a Double Pinwheel block to each end of the shorter pinwheel borders. Press.

3. Sew the top and bottom borders to the quilt, orienting the dark red border toward the center of the quilt. Press the seam allowance toward the navy blue border. *fig. H*

H Quilt assembly

FINISHING

Layer, quilt, and bind as desired.

Merry Snowmen by Jacki Montplaisar

Jacki chose the *Frosty Frolic* panel and coordinates from Wilmington Prints, and her version of this project gives it a completely different festive vibe!

Jacki chose a winter-themed panel and palette of fabrics. By simply turning the row of flag bunting at the top of the panel 180°, she turned it into half wreaths! At the bottom of the panel, the flags were also turned 180° and constructed from a strip set, giving them the appearance of trees.

A Bucketful of Sunshine

Design Suggestions

For my quilt, I chose to place the 28 flowers in the outer border in a scrappy fashion. The yardage listed is more than enough to accomplish a similar look. I've listed the cutting by color for **one** flower—you choose how many of each color you wish to make. Mix and match or make them all the same—the sky's the limit!

Swap the panel and switch up the color palette, and this quilt will easily work with any number of flower-focused panels! Try a complementary quilt block, such as the butterflies that Marie Clanton used in her quilt *Renewal* (page 31).

Luxuriate in the warm colors of fall with this vibrant quilt featuring fall leaves, pumpkins, and sunflowers. The Fall Is in the Air *panel and several complementary fabrics by Timeless Treasures combined with a scrappy selection of yellows, golds, and oranges make this a sunny quilt for fall decorating.*

Materials

Yardages are based on 41˝-wide fabric.

Panel: Single-image panel approximately 22½˝ × 40½˝.
I used *Fall Is in the Air* by Timeless Treasures.

Background: 2¾ yards

Green shimmer: ⅝ yard

Black shimmer: ⅞ yard

Brown: ⅜ yard

Deep red: ¼ yard

Gold: ⅜ yard

Yellow or dark yellow: ¼–½ yard of 8–15 fabrics

Variegated leaf print in tan, light orange, and dark orange:
1 yard for leaf blocks and outer coping strips

Striped: ⅝ yard for binding

Backing: 4¾ yards

Batting: 68˝ × 84˝ (twin)

Cutting

All block units will be subcut from the following pieces.

Background

Cut 2 strips 6½˝ × WOF (width of fabric).

Cut 6 strips 3½˝ × WOF.

Cut 4 strips 3˝ × WOF.

Cut 16 strips 2½˝ × WOF.

Cut 3 strips 2˝ × WOF.

Green Shimmer

Cut 1 strip 3˝ × WOF.

Cut 1 strip 2½˝ × WOF.

Cut 3 strips 2˝ × WOF.

Cut 5 strips 1½˝ × WOF.

Black Shimmer

Cut 4 strips 4½˝ × WOF.

Cut 1 strip 3˝ × WOF.

Cut 1 strip 2½˝ × WOF.

Brown

Cut 4 strips 1½˝ × WOF.

Cut 2 strips 1˝ × WOF.

Deep Red

Cut 1 strip 3˝ × WOF.

Cut 1 strip 2½˝ × WOF.

Yellow or Dark Yellow

Cut 6 strips 3½˝ × WOF.

Cut 1 strip 3˝ × WOF.

Cut 1 strip 2½˝ × WOF.

Cut 3 strips 1¾˝ × WOF.

Gold

Cut 1 strip 3˝ × WOF.

Cut 1 strip 2½˝ × WOF.

Cut 2 strips 1¾˝ × WOF.

Variegated Leaf Print

Cut 6 strips 3½˝ × WOF.

Cut 1 strip 3˝ × WOF.

Cut 4 strips 2½˝ × WOF.

Cut 2 strips 1¾˝ × WOF.

Cut 2 strips 1½˝ × WOF.

Striped

Cut 8 strips 2½˝ × WOF.

CONSTRUCTION

Before beginning any project, read the General Instructions (page 7). This project uses construction techniques for Snowball Corners (page 13), Half-Square Triangles (HSTs) (page 11), and Combination Triangle units (page 12).

Panel Preparation

Adjust your panel to 22½˝ × 40½˝. Be sure that the panel is squared up before you trim or add coping strips! See Squaring Up Panel Images (page 7).

CUTTING

Cut 2 brown coping strips 1½˝ × 40½˝.

Cut 2 brown coping strips 1½˝ × 24½˝.

ASSEMBLY

Press all seam allowances open unless otherwise noted.

1. Sew the 1½˝ × 40½˝ strips to the sides of the panel.

2. Sew the 1½˝ × 24½˝ strips to the top and bottom of the panel.

Maple Leaf Blocks

FINISHED BLOCK: 6˝ × 6˝

Make 2 blocks each of green, black, deep red, gold, tan, variegated (light orange and dark orange) for a total of 14.

CUTTING

Cut 42 background squares 3˝ × 3˝.

Cut 14 background squares 2½˝ × 2½˝.

Cut 14 brown-stem rectangles 1˝ × 5˝.

For each of the 14 Maple Leaf blocks:

Cut 2 color squares 3˝ × 3˝.

Cut 3 color squares 2½˝ × 2½˝.

ASSEMBLY

Press all seam allowances open unless otherwise noted.

1. Pair a colored square 3˝ × 3˝ with a background square 3˝ × 3˝ to construct 2 HSTs. Make 2 sets for a total of 4 HSTs per color. Press and trim to 2½˝ × 2½˝.

2. Using 1 background square 3˝ × 3˝ and one 1˝ × 5˝ stem rectangle, make the stem block by cutting the background square once on the diagonal. Line the rectangle up with the center of each triangle by folding the stem rectangle and each triangle in half and finger-pressing. Match the fold lines. Stitch each triangle onto either side of the stem rectangle. Trim this block to 2½˝ × 2½˝, centering the stem. *fig. A*

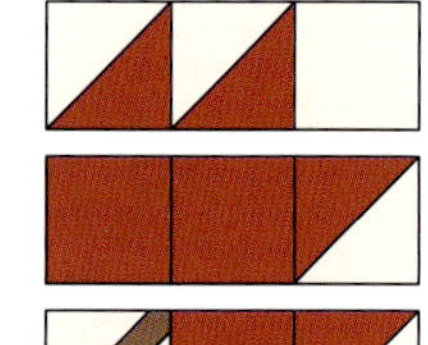

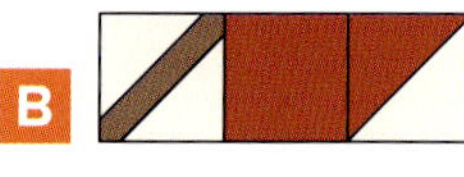

3. Lay out the block as shown and sew each row. Then, sew the 3 rows together. Press. *fig. B*

Maple Leaf Border

CUTTING

From **each** background strip 6½˝ × WOF, cut 1 background square 6½˝ × 6½˝ and 1 background strip 6½˝ × 30½˝.

ASSEMBLY

Press all seam allowances open unless otherwise noted.

1. Arrange 2 sets of 3 Maple Leaf blocks and a background square 6½˝ × 6½˝ as shown. *fig. C*

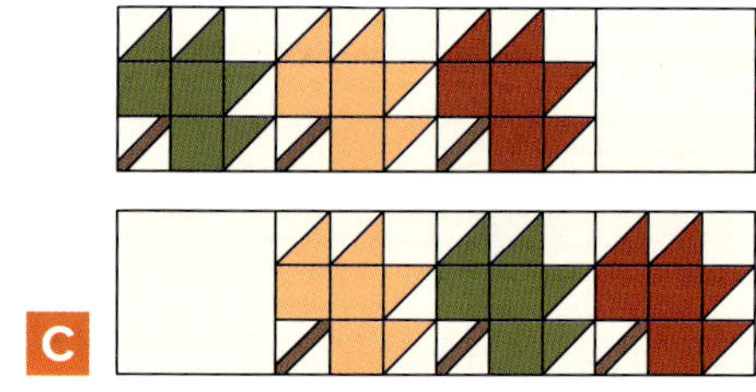

2. Sew each row together and press.

3. Sew the first row to the top of the panel and sew the second row to the bottom of the panel.

4. Arrange 2 sets of 4 Maple Leaf blocks and a background strip 6½˝ × 30½˝ as shown. *fig. D*

5. Sew each row together and press.

6. Sew the first row to the left side of the panel and sew the second row to the right side of the panel.

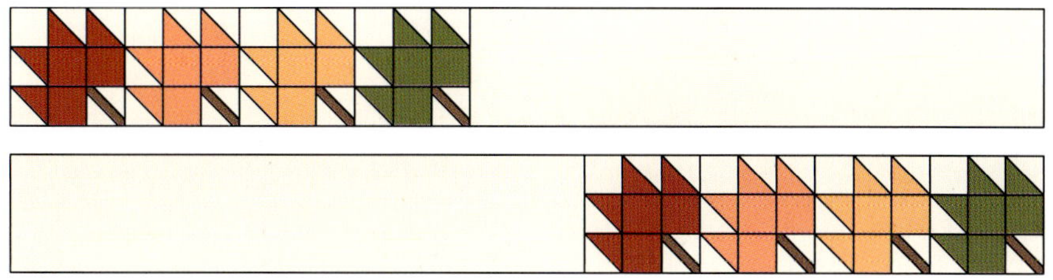

D

Outer Coping Strips

CUTTING

Cut 2 strips 1½˝ × 36½˝ from variegated leaf-print strips.

Subcut 1 variegated strip 2½˝ × WOF in half to create 2 pieces 2½˝ × 20˝.

ASSEMBLY

Press all seam allowances open unless otherwise noted.

1. Sew a variegated strip 1½˝ × 36½˝ to the top and bottom of the panel section.

2. Sew a variegated strip 2½˝ × 20˝ to each of the remaining 2½˝ × WOF variegated strips.

3. Trim the long 2½˝ × 60½˝ variegated strips to 2½˝ × 56½˝.

4. Sew the 2½˝ × 56½˝ strips to the sides of the panel section.

Sunflower Blocks

FINISHED BLOCK: 8˝ × 8˝

Make 28.

CUTTING LEAF AND CENTER UNITS

Cut 28 black squares 4½˝ × 4½˝ for the flower centers; subcut 112 rectangles 1½˝ × 2½˝ from the 2½˝ × WOF background strips.

Cut 56 green squares 2˝ × 2˝.

Cut 112 green squares 1½˝ × 1½˝.

Cut 56 background squares 2˝ × 2˝.

Cut 28 sets of 4 gold, orange, dark yellow, or yellow squares 1¾˝ × 1¾˝ for each flower center.

ASSEMBLY

Press all seam allowances open unless otherwise noted.

1. Sew a gold square 1¾˝ × 1¾˝ onto each corner of the center black 4½˝ × 4½˝ squares by using the Snowball Corners technique (page 13). *fig. E*

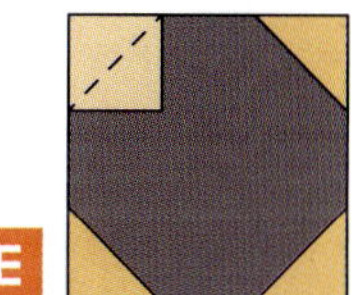

2. Pair a green square 2˝ × 2˝ with a background square 2˝ × 2˝ to make 2 HSTs. Repeat for a total of 112 HSTs. Press and trim to 1½˝ × 1½˝.

3. Sew a green square 1½˝ × 1½˝ to a HST completed in Step 1, oriented as illustrated. Press the seam allowance toward the green square. Make 56. *fig. F*

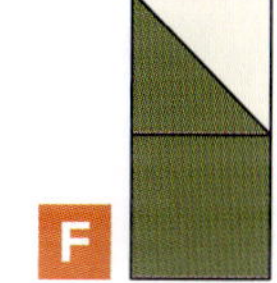

4. Sew each of the remaining 56 HSTs to a green square 1½˝ × 1½˝, oriented as illustrated. Press the seam allowance toward the green square. *fig. G*

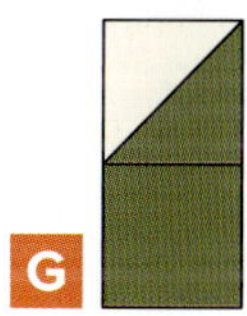

5. Sew a background rectangle 1½˝ × 2½˝ to the left side of the 56 units made in Step 3. Sew a background rectangle 1½˝ × 1½˝ to the right side of the 56 remaining leaf units. Be sure your HSTs are oriented correctly! Press the seams toward the rectangle. Set aside. *fig. H*

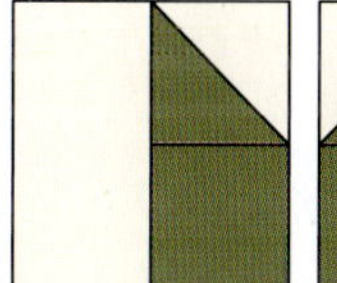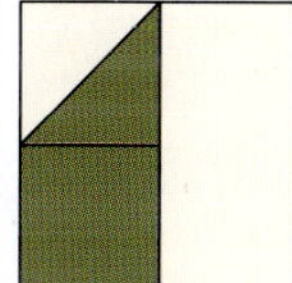

CUTTING FLOWER PETALS

I selected a variety of colors for my flowers; see the design suggestions at the beginning of this project for ideas. For **each** of the 28 flower blocks:

Cut 2 background squares 3½˝ × 3½˝.

Cut 2 orange (or color of your choice) squares 3½˝ × 3½˝.

Cut 2 dark yellow (or color of your choice) squares 3½˝ × 3½˝.

FLOWER PETALS ASSEMBLY

1. Pair a dark yellow square 3½˝ × 3½˝ and a background square 3½˝ × 3½˝ to sew 2 HSTs. Cut in half and press. **Do not trim.** Make 2 for a total of 4 HSTs.

2. Pair each of the HSTs from Step 1 with an orange square 3½˝ × 3½˝ to construct 8 Combination Triangle units:
4 units will face left, and 4 will face right. Press and trim to 2½˝ × 2½˝. *fig. I*

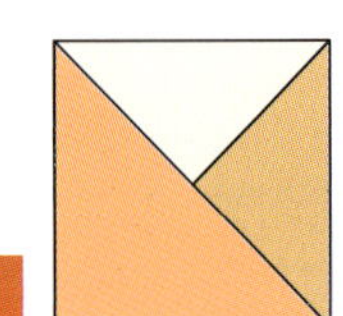
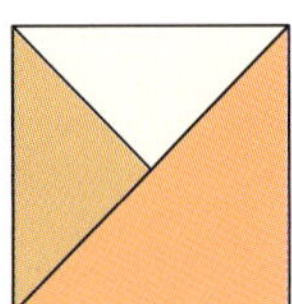

TIP

Be sure to check the general instructions for Combination Triangle units (page 12) for how to trim these units correctly!

3. Sew left and right pairs of Combination Triangle units together to form a Flying Geese (FG) variation unit.

4. Lay out the block as illustrated and stitch together. Press. *fig. J*

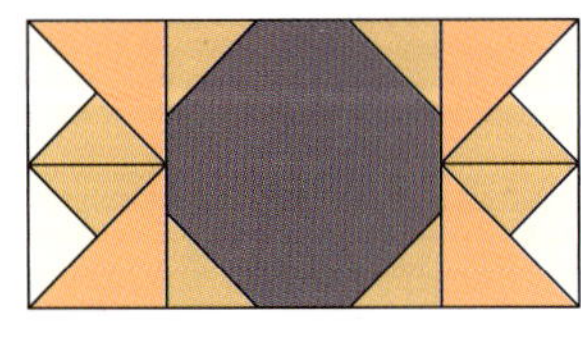

5. Repeat Steps 1–4 to make 28 Sunflower blocks.

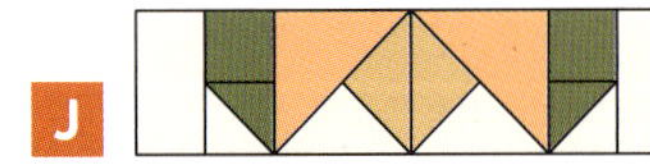

CUTTING THE SUNFLOWER BORDER

Cut 28 background rectangles 2½˝ × 8½˝.

Cut 4 background rectangles 2½˝ × 10½˝.

SUNFLOWER BORDER ASSEMBLY

Press all seam allowances open unless otherwise noted.

1. Add a background rectangle 2½˝ × 8½˝ to the top of each Sunflower block. *fig. K*

2. Arrange 5 blocks as shown for the top border, rotating the alternate blocks.

3. Sew together and press. *fig. L*

4. Repeat Steps 2–3 to make the bottom border.

5. Add these borders to the top and bottom of your quilt.

6. Arrange 9 blocks as shown, rotating the alternate blocks, to make the left and right borders. *fig. M*

7. Sew a background rectangle 2½˝ × 10½˝ to both ends of each side border. *fig. N*

8. Sew these borders to the left and right sides of your quilt, paying attention to which border is sewn to the left or right side. Refer to the photo (page 26).

FINISHING

1. Quilt, bind, and add a hanging sleeve, if desired.

2. Enjoy!

Make It Your Own

Renewal by Marie Clanton

Marie chose the *Spring Song* panel and an assortment of coordinates by Timeless Treasures and added a variety of colorful scraps from her stash to create this vibrant quilt. She also replaced the Maple Leaf blocks with a Butterfly block (page 32) to emphasize the spring theme.

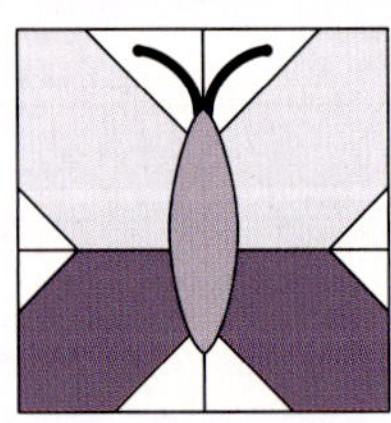

Optional Butterfly Block

FINISHED BLOCK: 6″ × 6″

Cutting

Cut 2 light purple rectangles 3½″ × 4″.

Cut 2 dark purple rectangles 3″ × 3½″.

Cut 2 background squares A 2⅜″ × 2⅜″.

Cut 4 background squares B 1½″ × 1½″.

Cut 2 background squares C 1⅞″ × 1⅞″.

Cut 1 butterfly body by using the Butterfly Body template (page 124).

ASSEMBLY

Press all seam allowances open unless otherwise noted.

1. Sew a 2⅜″ × 2⅜″ background square A to the upper-right corner of a light purple rectangle 3½″ × 4″ to make a Snowball Corner (page 13), being sure to orient the rectangle with the 3½″ edge horizontally and the 4″ edge vertically. Press the seam allowance toward the background corner.

2. Sew a 1½″ × 1½″ background square B to the lower-left corner of a light purple rectangle to make a Snowball Corner opposite from the first Snowball Corner. Press the seam allowance toward the background corner. *A*

3. Repeat Steps 1–2 with a second light purple rectangle, placing Snowball Corner A in the upper-left corner of the rectangle and Snowball Corner B in the lower-right corner of the rectangle. Press the seam allowance toward the background corner. *B*

4. Sew a 1½″ × 1½″ background square B to the upper-left corner of a dark purple rectangle 3″ × 3½″ to make a Snowball Corner, being sure to orient the rectangle with the 3½″ edge horizontally and the 3″ edge vertically. Press the seam allowance toward the background corner.

5. Sew a background square C 1⅞″ × 1⅞″ to the lower-right corner of the rectangle from Step 4 to make a Snowball Corner. Press the seam allowance toward the corner. *C*

6. Repeat Steps 4–5 with a second dark purple rectangle, placing Snowball Corner B in the upper-right corner of the rectangle and Snowball Corner C in the lower-left corner of the rectangle. Press the seam allowance toward the corner. *D*

7. Arrange the rectangles as shown, matching the Snowball Corners, and sew together. Press.

8. Sew the rows together and press. *E*

9. Appliqué a butterfly body over the center seam as shown.

10. Embroider antennae to the top of the butterfly body, if desired.

Santa's Coming!

FINISHED QUILT: 64″ × 70″

Design Suggestions

A variety of solo panels are wider than usual, and this project was a fun opportunity to work with one of those. It is fairly easy to adapt this project and tone down the folk-art feel. Substitute the houses with traditional Star blocks or other themed blocks to personalize the project to your panel! See how Laura Tanner stylized her quilt *Not a Creature Was Stirring* (page 42) and the adjustments she made to the instructions to make it work.

The holidays are filled with magic for youngsters of all ages. The story of Santa coming down the chimney with a sack of toys has always been one of my favorites. I used the Riley Blake panel Up on the Housetop *and coordinating fabrics to create the quirky trees, the Dresden wreath, stars, hearts, and houses to give this project a folk-art feel.*

Materials

Yardages are based on 41˝-wide fabric.

Panel: Single-image panel approximately 36˝ × 43˝. I used *Up on the Housetop* by Riley Blake.

Cream for background: 2⅜ yards

Coordinating solids and prints: ¼–½ yard each of 8–12 fabrics for patchwork and appliqué

Dark green: ⅝ yard for checkerboard, frame, and trees

Red: ¼ yard for appliqué hearts

Gold: ¼ yard for appliqué stars

Binding: ⅝ yard

Backing: 4⅛ yards

Batting: 72˝ × 78˝ (twin)

Dresden Plate blade template (page 121) or EZ Quilting Easy Dresden Ruler by Darlene Zimmerman

Large Star and Heart templates (pages 122–123)

Circle template (page 122)

Tree and Tree Trunk templates (page 122)

Cutting

Cream

Cut 2 strips 14½˝ × WOF (width of fabric).

Cut 1 strip 6½˝ × WOF.

Cut 2 strips 6˝ × WOF.

Cut 1 strip 3½˝ × WOF.

Cut 9 strips 2½˝ × WOF.

Cut 3 strips 2˝ × WOF.

Dark Green

Cut 7 strips 2½˝ × WOF.

Binding

Cut 7 strips 2½˝ × WOF.

CONSTRUCTION

Before beginning any project, read the General Instructions (page 7). This project uses construction techniques for Half-Square Triangles (HSTs) (page 11), Strip Sets (page 13), and Flying Geese (FG) units (page 13).

Panel Preparation

Adjust the panel to 30½˝ × 34½˝. Be sure that it is squared up! See Squaring Up Panel Images (page 7) to adjust your panel to fit into the design.

CUTTING

Cut 4 dark green coping strips 2½˝ × 34½˝.

ASSEMBLY

Press all seam allowances open unless otherwise noted.

1. Sew a dark green 2½˝ × 34½˝ strip to each side of the central panel.

2. Sew a dark green 2½˝ × 34½˝ strip to the top and bottom of the central panel.

Checkerboard Borders

1. Sew a strip set pairing a cream strip 2½″ × WOF with a dark green strip 2½″ × WOF. Make 3. Press the seam allowance toward the dark green strip.

2. Subcut each strip set 2½″ × 4½″ to create 36 pairs of dark green and cream rectangles. *fig. A*

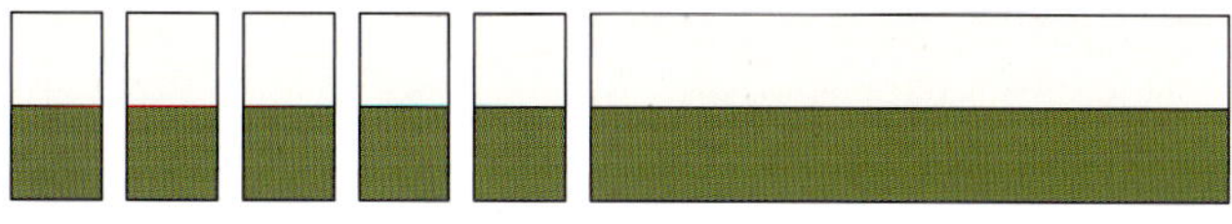

A

3. Sew 8 pairs end to end beginning with green, plus 1 green square 2½″ × 2½″ on the end to make the top and bottom borders. *fig. B*

B 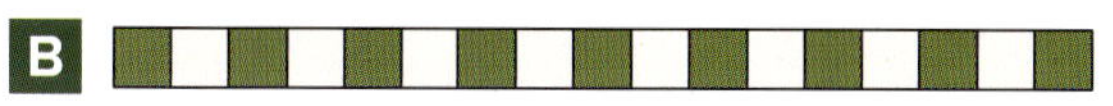

4. Sew 10 pairs end to end beginning with a cream square, plus 1 cream square 2½″ × 2½″ to make the side borders. *fig. C*

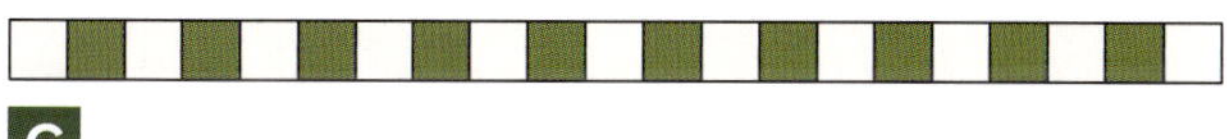

C

5. Sew the top and bottom borders to the central panel, pressing toward the frame.

6. Sew the side borders to the central panel, pressing toward the frame strips.

Large Tree Borders

CUTTING

Cut 4 cream squares 6½″ × 6½″.

Cut 4 cream rectangles 6″ × 13½″.

Cut 4 cream rectangles 3½″ × 6½″.

Cut 4 cream squares 3½″ × 3½″.

Cut 2 cream squares 3″ × 3″.

Cut 4 cream rectangles 2½″ × 6½″.

Cut 4 cream rectangles 2½″ × 4½″.

Cut 60 cream squares 2½″ × 2½″.

Cut 8 cream rectangles 2″ × 5″.

Cut 4 cream rectangles 2″ × 3½″.

Cut 24 cream squares 2″ × 2″.

Cut 60 coordinating-color squares 2½″ × 2½″.

Cut 2 dark brown strips 1½″ × 31½″.

Cut 2 dark brown squares 3″ × 3″.

Use the Star template (page 122) to cut 2 red stars for the appliqué method of your choice.

ASSEMBLY

Press all seam allowances open unless otherwise noted.

1. Pair a cream square 2½″ × 2½″ and a colored square 2½″ × 2½″ to make 2 HSTs. Repeat to make 60 HSTs per tree, for a total of 120. Mix the colored squares for a scrappy look. Press and trim to 2″ × 2″.

2. Pair a dark brown square 3″ × 3″ and a cream square 3″ × 3″ to make 2 HSTs. Make 4. Press and trim to 2½″ × 2½″. Set aside for the Trees Assembly step (page 36).

Tree Section 1

1. Lay out 6 HSTs 2″ × 2″ and 2 cream squares 2″ × 2″; sew each of the 4 rows for the right side of Section 1. Press.

2. Sew a cream rectangle 3½″ × 6½″ to the right side of the rows from Step 1. Press the seam allowance toward the rectangle. *fig. D*

D 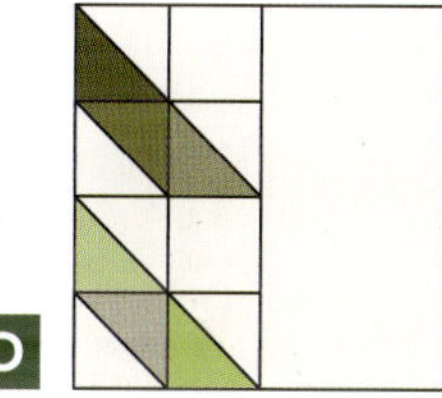

3. Construct a mirror image of these units for the left side of Section 1. *fig. E*

E 

Tree Section 2

1. Lay out 8 HSTs 2″ × 2″ and a cream square 2″ × 2″; sew each of the 3 rows for the right side of Section 2. Press.

2. Sew a cream rectangle 2″ × 5″ to the right side of the rows from Step 1. Press the seam allowance toward the rectangle. *fig. F*

F 

3. Construct a mirror image of these units for the left side of Section 2. *fig. G*

G 

Tree Section 3

Lay out 2 sets of 4 HSTs 2″ × 2″ to construct a right and a left Section 3 unit. Sew each unit together and press. *fig. A*

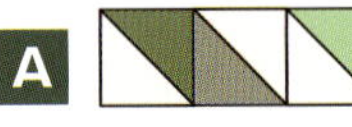 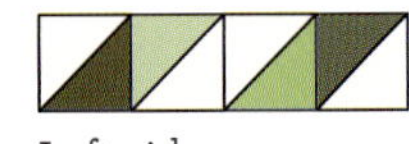

Right side   Left side

Tree Section 4

1. Lay out 3 HSTs 2″ × 2″ and a cream square 2″ × 2″; sew the 2 rows for the right side of Section 4. Press.

2. Sew a cream square 3½″ × 3½″ to the right side of Section 4. Press the seam allowance toward the square.

3. Construct a mirror image of these units for the left side. *fig. B*

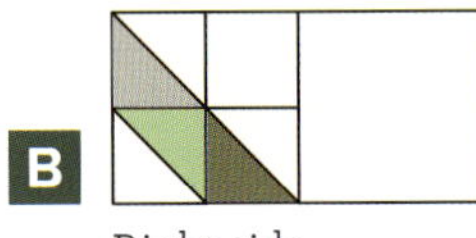 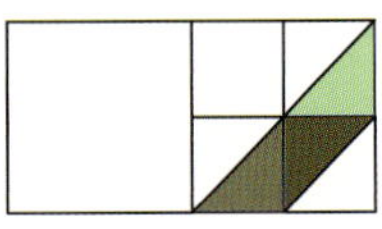

Right side   Left side

Tree Section 5

1. Lay out 7 HSTs 2″ × 2″ and 2 cream squares 2″ × 2″; sew the 3 rows for the right side of Section 5. Press.

2. Sew a cream rectangle 2″ × 5″ to the right side of Section 5. Press the seam allowance toward the rectangle.

3. Construct a mirror image of these units for the left side of Section 5. *fig. C*

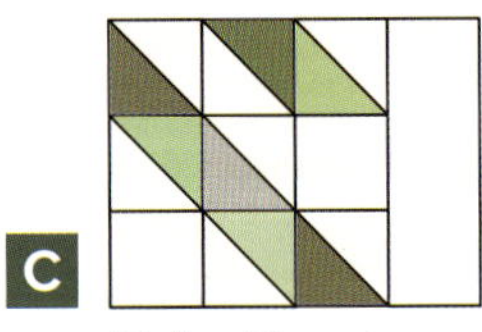 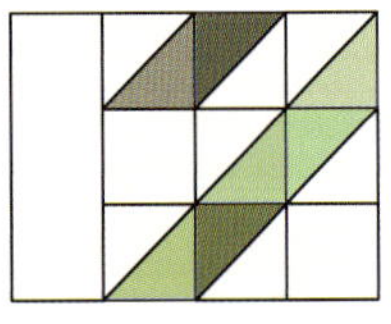

Right side   Left side

Tree Section 6

Lay out 2 HSTs 2″ × 2″ and a cream rectangle 2″ × 3½″; construct a left and right Section 6. Sew together and press the seam allowance toward the rectangle. *fig. D*

 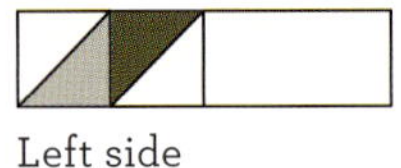

Right side   Left side

Trees Assembly

1. Sew the right side of the tree together, with Section 1 at the top and Section 6 at the bottom. Sew the left-side sections together in the same manner. Press. *fig. E*

Right side   Left side

2. Sew a cream square 6½″ × 6½″ to the bottom of both the left and right sections constructed in Step 1. Press the seam allowance toward the square.

3. Sew a cream rectangle 2½″ × 6½″ to the top of each Section 1. Press the seam allowance toward the rectangle.

4. Sew a brown/cream HST 2½″ × 2½″ to a cream rectangle 2½″ × 4½″. Make 2, paying close attention to the orientation of the HST. *fig. F*

Right side   Left side

5. Sew the unit made in Step 4 to the bottom of the left and right sides of the tree. Press the seam allowance toward the cream square 6½˝ × 6½˝.

6. Sew the dark brown strip 1½˝ × 31½˝ to the right edge of the left side of the tree. Press the seam allowance toward the brown strip. Sew the right half of the tree to the other side of the brown strip, being sure that the tree branches are facing the correct direction. *fig. G*

G

7. Sew a cream rectangle 6˝ × 13½˝ to both the top and bottom of the tree. Press the seam allowance toward the rectangle.

8. Appliqué a star to the top of each tree.

9. Sew a tree border to each side of the central panel. *fig. H*

H

10. Repeat Tree Sections 1–6 (pages 35–36) and Assemble the Tree (pages 36–37) to make the second tree.

Top Border

CUTTING

Cut 6 red hearts and 10 gold stars by using the Heart and Large Star templates (pages 122 and 123) and prepare them for the appliqué method of your choice.

Cut 20 strips 4½˝ × 3˝ from assorted colors for the Dresden Plate; subcut 20 blades from the 4½˝ × 3˝ strips by using the Dresden Plate blade template (page 121) or the EZ Quilting Easy Dresden Ruler by Darlene Zimmerman.

Using the Circle template (page 122), cut 1 circle for the appliqué center of the Dresden Plate. If your chosen appliqué method requires fusible interfacing, apply that now.

DRESDEN PLATE ASSEMBLY

1. Following the instructions for Dresden Plates (page 14), stitch 20 blades together to form a Dresden Plate.

2. Appliqué the circle onto the center of the Dresden Plate. *fig. A*

TOP BORDER ASSEMBLY

1. Sew together 2 cream strips 14˝ × WOF and trim to 14˝ × 64½˝.

2. Mark the center of the border and the center of the Dresden Plate.

3. Appliqué the Dresden Plate, stars, and hearts to the border, placing the stars and hearts as desired. *fig. B*

4. Sew the top border to the central panel section.

Bottom Border

The houses are constructed from the 8–12 coordinating prints and solids in the supply list. No specific colors are given below. Feel free to select colors that best suit your panel and quilt.

HOUSE 1
FINISHED SIZE: 12˝ × 14˝

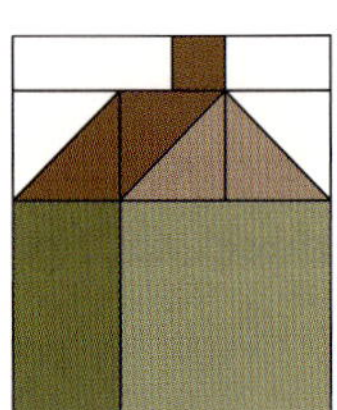

Cutting

Cut 1 house side rectangle 4½˝ × 8½˝.

Cut 1 house front square 8½˝ × 8½˝.

Cut 2 side roof squares 5˝ × 5˝.

Cut 2 front roof squares 5˝ × 5˝.

Cut 2 cream squares 5˝ × 5˝.

Cut 1 chimney square 2½˝ × 2½˝.

Cut 1 cream rectangle 2½˝ × 6½˝.

Cut 1 cream rectangle 2½˝ × 4½˝.

House 1 Assembly

1. Stitch the house side 4½˝ × 8½˝ to the left side of the house front 8½˝ × 8½˝. Press the seam allowance toward the house square.

2. Pair a cream square 5˝ × 5˝ with a dark brown square 5˝ × 5˝ to make 2 HSTs. Press and trim to 4½˝ × 4½˝.

3. Pair a dark brown square 5˝ × 5˝ and a light brown square 5˝ × 5˝ to make 2 HSTs. Press and trim to 4½˝ × 4½˝.

4. Pair a cream square 5˝ × 5˝ and a light brown square 5˝ × 5˝ to make 2 HSTs. Press and trim to 4½˝ × 4½˝.

5. Sew a cream/dark brown HST to the left side of a dark brown/light brown HST. Press.

6. Sew a light brown/cream HST to the right side of a dark brown/light brown HST to create the roof row. Discard the remaining HSTs. *fig. C*

7. Sew a cream rectangle 2½˝ × 6½˝ to a dark brown square 2½˝ × 2½˝. Press the seam allowance toward the square.

8. Sew a cream rectangle 2½″ × 4½″ to make the sky row.

9. Sew the 3 rows together and press.

HOUSE 2
FINISHED SIZE: 14″ × 14″

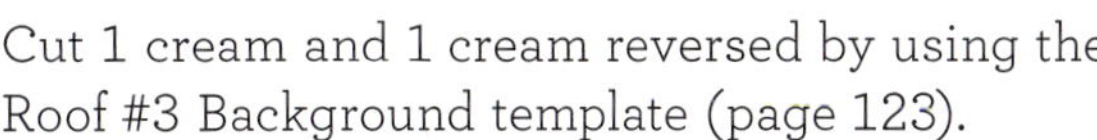

Cutting

Cut 2 house front rectangles 6½″ × 7½″.

Cut 1 house rectangle 2½″ × 3½″.

Cut 1 door rectangle 2½″ × 4½″.

Cut 1 cream square 5½″ × 5½″.

Cut 1 roof square 5½″ × 5½″.

Cut 1 roof rectangle 4½″ × 6½″.

Cut 1 cream rectangle 3½″ × 14½″.

House 2 Assembly

1. Pair a roof square 5½″ × 5½″ and a cream square 5½″ × 5½″ to make 2 HSTs. Press and trim to 4½″ × 4½″.

2. Sew a roof rectangle 4½″ × 6½″ between the 2 HSTs from Step 1, orienting the HST. *fig. D*

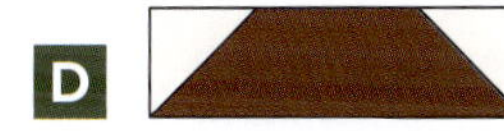

3. Sew the house rectangle 2½″ × 3½″ to the top of the door rectangle 2½″ × 4½″. Press the seam allowance toward the house rectangle.

4. Sew the house rectangles 6½″ × 7½″ to both sides of the door unit. Press the seam allowances toward the house rectangles. *fig. E*

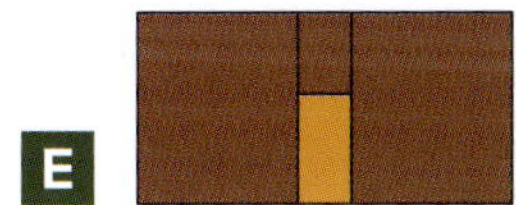

5. Sew the roof to the house. Press the seam allowance toward the house.

6. Sew the cream rectangle 3½″ × 14½″ to the top of the house. Press the seam allowance toward the roof.

HOUSE 3
FINISHED SIZE: 8″ × 14″

Cutting

Cut 1 roof triangle using the Roof #3 template (page 123).

Cut 1 cream and 1 cream reversed by using the Roof #3 Background template (page 123).

Cut 2 house rectangles 3½″ × 8½″.

Cut 1 house color rectangle 2½″ × 4½″.

Cut 1 door color rectangle 2½″ × 4½″.

House 3 Assembly

1. On the wrong side of the fabric, mark registration points of the Roof #3 triangle and Roof #3 Background and reversed background triangle. Match the registration points and sew the cream pieces to the roof triangle. Press the seam allowances toward the triangles. *fig. F*

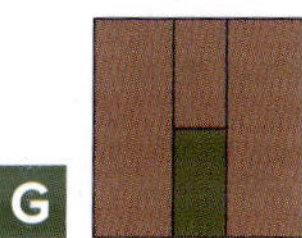

2. Sew the house rectangle 2½″ × 4½″ to the top of the door rectangle 2½″ × 4½″ along the short edge. Press the seam allowance toward the house rectangle.

3. Sew a house rectangle 3½″ × 8½″ to each side of the door unit. Press the seam allowance toward the house rectangles. *fig. G*

4. Sew the roof to the top of the house. Press the seam allowance toward the house.

HOUSE 4

FINISHED SIZE: 6″ × 14″

Cutting

Cut 1 house rectangle 6½″ × 8½″.

Cut 1 roof rectangle 3½″ × 6½″.

Cut 2 cream squares 3½″ × 3½″.

Cut 1 cream rectangle 3½″ × 6½″.

House 4 Assembly

1. Sew a cream 3½″ × 3½″ square to each side of the roof rectangle 3½″ × 6½″ to construct 1 FG unit.

2. Sew the roof to the top of the house rectangle 6½″ × 8½″. Press the seam allowance toward the rectangle.

3. Sew the 3½″ × 6½″ cream rectangle to the top of the FG unit.

HOUSE 5

FINISHED SIZE: 14″ × 14″

Cutting

Cut 1 front roof rectangle 3½″ × 6½″.

Cut 1 house front rectangle 6½″ × 8½″.

Cut 2 house side rectangles 3½″ × 8½″.

Cut 2 house side rectangles 1½″ × 2½″.

Cut 1 house side square 2½″ × 2½″.

Cut 2 window squares 2½″ × 2½″.

Cut 2 chimney squares 2½″ × 2½″.

Cut 1 cream square 4″ × 4″.

Cut 1 cream rectangle 3½″ × 4½″.

Cut 3 cream squares 3½″ × 3½″.

Cut 2 cream rectangles 1½″ × 2½″.

Cut 2 side roof squares 4″ × 4″.

Cut 1 side roof rectangle 3½″ × 5½″.

Cut 1 side roof square 3½″ × 3½″.

House 5 Assembly

1. Use the front roof 3½″ × 6½″ rectangle, a cream 3½″ × 3½″ square, and the side roof 3½″ × 3½″ square to make an FG for the roof.

2. Pair a cream square 4″ × 4″ and the side roof square 4″ × 4″ to make 2 HSTs. Press and trim to 3½″ × 3½″. Discard 1 HST.

3. Arrange the units from Steps 1–2 with the side roof rectangle 3½″ × 5½″ and sew together. Press the seam allowance toward the rectangle. *fig. H* 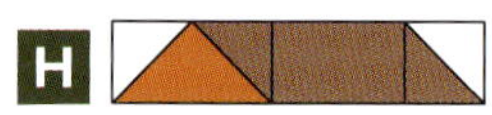

4. Arrange 2 house rectangles 1½″ × 2½″, 2 window squares 2½″ × 2½″, and a house square 2½″ × 2½″ as shown. Sew together and press the seam allowances toward the window squares.

5. Sew a house rectangle 3½″ × 8½″ to the top and bottom of the window row. *fig. I* 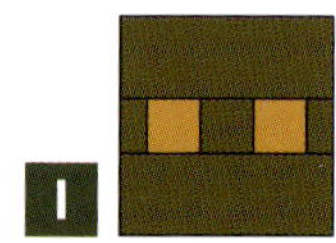

6. Sew the house side rectangle 6½″ × 8½″ to the left side of the Step 5 main house section. Press the seam allowance toward the house side rectangle. *fig. J* 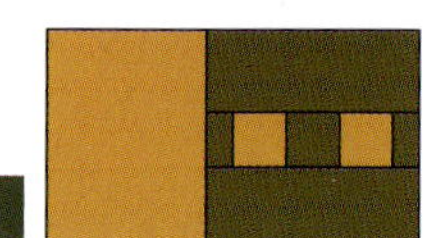

7. Sew a cream rectangle 1½″ × 2½″ to the top of each chimney 1½″ × 1½″ square to make 2 chimney units. Press the seam allowance toward the chimneys.

8. Sew a cream square 3½″ × 3½″ to the left of a chimney unit. Sew a second cream square 3½″ × 3½″ to the right of the second chimney unit. Press the seam allowances toward the cream squares.

9. Sew a cream rectangle 3½″ × 4½″ between the left and right chimney units. Press the seam allowance toward the cream rectangle. *fig. K* 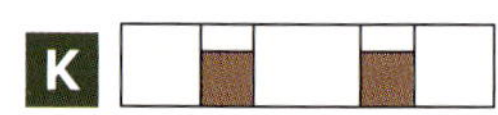

10. Sew the chimney row to the top of the Step 3 roof row and then sew this unit to the top of the house body.

SMALL TREE BLOCKS

FINISHED SIZE: 4″ × 14″

Make 2.

Cutting

Cut 2 cream rectangles 4½″ × 14½″.

Cut 2 trees to appliqué by using the Tree template (page 122).

Cut 2 tree trunks to appliqué by using the Tree Trunk template (page 122).

Small Tree Block Assembly

1. Using the appliqué method of your choice, appliqué tree trunks to a cream rectangle 4½″ × 14½″, aligning the centers and placing the trunk about 1½″ up from the lower edge.

2. Appliqué the tree body to the cream rectangle 4½″ × 14½″, matching the center of the tree to the center of the block.

BOTTOM BORDER ASSEMBLY

Cutting

Cut 2 cream rectangles 1½″ × 14½″.

1. Arrange 2 cream rectangles 1½″ × 14½″, houses 1–5, and 2 tree blocks as shown.

2. Sew together and press the seam allowances between the houses open. Press the seam allowances at the trees and the ends toward the background.

3. Sew the house border to the bottom of the quilt.

FINISHING

Layer and quilt as desired.

FINISHED QUILT: 65″ × 76″

Not a Creature Was Stirring by Laura Tanner

Christmas Wishes panel from Riley Blake

Laura chose to make a variation of this pattern by using the *Christmas Wishes* panel and several coordinates from Riley Blake. Because her panel was longer, she added to the length of the frame around the panel and the checkerboard border, and she put an additional section on the tree. She also added another star to the top border. Instead of the house row, she added a row of stars with spacers in between. This is a great example of how to use the pattern and change it up a bit to give it your personal flair!

PROJECTS FOR UNIFORM-SIZE MULTI-IMAGE PANELS

Uniform-size multi-image panels are abundant, and each of the three projects presented here will provide you with inspiration to grab one of these gems and explore the fun of creating a beautiful quilt focused on the theme and colors of the panel you choose.

I have chosen to focus the projects on 4˝ and 6˝ panel images, but you will see from the contributor quilts that they can easily be adapted for other size images with a little simple math. There are even helpful charts demonstrating how to increase the sizes of the surrounding units.

It's also fairly easy to create a quilt by using fewer or more panel images, so don't let that slow you down. Stretch your imagination a little and add another row if you want more images or add another block to the rows you already have. You'll have to do some math to increase the size of your borders, but it will be worth the effort!

Besties

Design Suggestions

I made this quilt from the *Peter Rabbit and Friends* panel and coordinates by Riley Blake. I chose this panel because it has so many images, and they were the perfect size to fit in a 6″ × 6″ space created in the two blocks featured in the quilt. Storm at Sea and Sawtooth Star blocks lend themselves perfectly to featuring a panel in the center. Adding rows is a simple way to increase the size of this quilt. Take a look at *Splish Splash* (page 50) created by Adam Holladay to see how he used a fabric panel meant to be a soft-cover book and added extra rows to make this quilt his own!

Overlapping Storm at Sea and Sawtooth Star blocks feature Peter Rabbit and Friends in this cozy quilt, perfect for a special youngster in your life. The illusion of the overlapping blocks is achieved through an unusual sashing treatment.

Materials

Yardages are based on 41˝-wide fabrics.

Panel: Multi-image panel with uniform-size images adjustable to 6½˝ × 6½˝. I used *Peter Rabbit and Friends* by Riley Blake.

Cream for background: 4½ yards

Green text print: 1⅜ yards

Mint green: ⅜ yard

Soft pink: ⅜ yard

Medium blue: ⅜ yard

Light blue plaid: ⅜ yard

Medium pink: ⅜ yard

Green floral: ¾ yard each

Binding: ⅝ yard pink

Backing: 5¼ yards

Batting: 69˝ × 88˝

Cutting

All squares, rectangles, diamonds, and setting triangles will be cut from the following strips.

Cream

Cut 5 strips 6½˝ × WOF (width of fabric).

Cut 8 strips 4˝ × WOF.

Cut 6 strips 3⅝˝ × WOF.

Cut 9 strips 3½˝ × WOF.

Cut 7 strips 2⅞˝ × WOF.

Cut 4 strips 2⅝˝ × WOF.

Cut 3 strips 1½˝ × WOF.

Green Text

Cut 3 strips 4˝ × WOF.

Cut 7 strips 3½˝ × WOF.

Cut 2 strips 2⅞˝ × WOF.

Mint Green

Cut 1 strip 3½˝ × WOF.

Cut 1 strip 2⅞˝ × WOF.

Cut 1 strip 2⅝˝ × WOF.

Soft Pink

Cut 1 strip 3½˝ × WOF.

Cut 1 strip 2⅞˝ × WOF.

Cut 1 strip 2⅝˝ × WOF.

Medium Blue

Cut 1 strip 3½˝ × WOF.

Cut 1 strip 2⅞˝ × WOF.

Cut 1 strip 2⅝˝ × WOF.

Light Blue Plaid

Cut 1 strip 3½˝ × WOF.

Cut 1 strip 2⅞˝ × WOF.

Cut 1 strip 2⅝˝ × WOF.

Medium Pink

Cut 1 strip 3½˝ × WOF.

Cut 1 strip 2⅞˝ × WOF.

Cut 1 strip 2⅝˝ × WOF.

Green Floral

Cut 1 strip 3½˝ × WOF.

Cut 1 strip 2⅞˝ × WOF.

Cut 1 strip 2⅝˝ × WOF.

Cut 7 strips 2˝ × WOF.

Binding

Cut 8 strips 2½˝ × WOF.

CONSTRUCTION

Before beginning any project, read the General Instructions (page 7). This project uses construction techniques for Flying Geese (FG) units (page 13) as well as Square in a Square and Diamond Recs blocks, illustrated within the pattern.

Panel Preparation

Adjust 18 panel images to 6½˝ × 6½˝. See Panel Preparation (page 7) for how to adjust the panel images to this size.

Storm at Sea Blocks

FINISHED BLOCK: 12˝ × 12˝

Make 2 each mint green, soft pink, medium blue, light blue plaid, medium pink, and green floral, for a total of 12.

Substitute the colors above for the diamonds and squares listed below as soft pink.

CUTTING

Cut 4 soft pink diamonds from the 3½˝ × WOF strip by using the Storm at Sea Diamond template (page 124).

Cut 8 background pairs of setting triangles from the background 4˝ × WOF strip by using the Storm at Sea 3˝ Diamond Setting triangle template (page 124).

Cut 2 soft pink squares 2⅞˝ × 2⅞˝; subcut each square once on the diagonal.

Cut 2 green text squares 2⅞˝ × 2⅞˝; subcut each square once on the diagonal.

Cut 4 background squares 2⅝˝ × 2⅝˝.

> **NOTE** Notice how I left out the central Square in a Square units from traditional Storm at Sea blocks to create space for the panel images and how I recolored the corner Square in a Square block to create the sashing variation of the Sawtooth Star.

ASSEMBLY

Press all seam allowances open unless otherwise noted.

1. Mark a registration point on the wrong side of each diamond at the ¼˝ seam allowance in each of the 4 points of the diamond, as indicated on the template. Mark a registration point on the wrong side of the setting triangles, as indicated on the template.

2. Pair a soft pink diamond with 2 setting triangles on the upper-left and lower-right sides of the diamond, being sure to match registration points. Stitch and press the seam allowance toward the setting triangles. *fig. A*

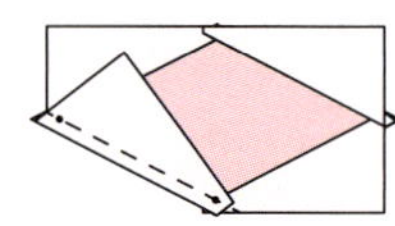

3. Pair 2 setting triangles to the upper right and lower left, being sure to match registration points. Stitch and press the seam allowance toward the setting triangles. Trim away all points from the edges of the unit. Make 4. *fig. B*

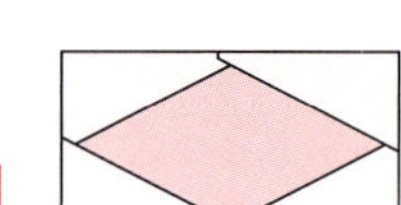

4. Sew a soft pink triangle cut from the 2⅞˝ × 2⅞˝ square to one side of the background square 2⅝˝ × 2⅝˝. Press the seam allowance toward the triangle. *fig. C*

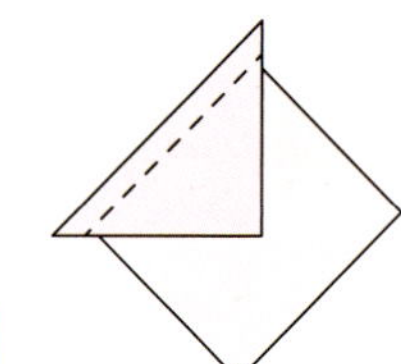

5. Sew a green text triangle cut from the 2⅞˝ × 2⅞˝ square on the opposite side of the background square 2⅝˝ × 2⅝˝. Press the seam allowance toward the triangle. *fig. D*

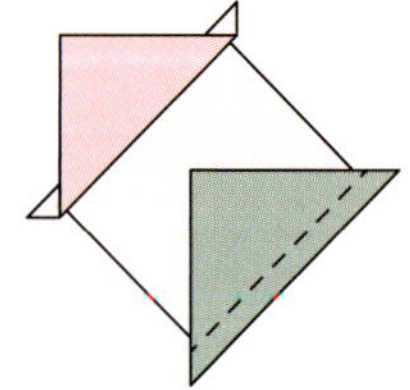

6. Sew a background triangle cut from the 2⅞″ × 2⅞″ square to 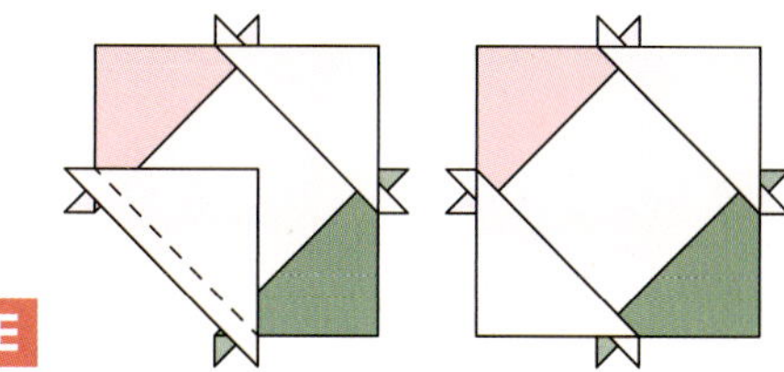 the remaining 2 sides of the center square. Press the seam allowance toward the triangles. Trim off the dog ears. *fig. E*

TIP

The 4 corner blocks in the quilt body do not have green triangles on the outer corner Square in a Square block. They have 1 color triangle to coordinate with the Storm at Sea block and the 3 background triangles; refer to the quilt photo at the beginning of this project.

7. Lay out the block as illustrated, with the panel image in the center. Sew each row, pressing seam allowances open on the top and bottom rows and pressing toward the panel image in the center row. *fig. F*

8. Sew the rows together and press.

9. Make 8 blocks as shown and 4 blocks for the quilt corners with a background corner at the outer corner. *fig. G*

Sawtooth Star Sashing

FLYING GEESE UNITS
FINISHED SIZE: 3″ × 6″

Make 34.

Cutting

Cut 34 cream rectangles 3½″ × 6½″ from the background 3½″ × WOF strips.

Cut 68 green text squares 3½″ × 3½″.

Assembly

Following the instructions in Flying Geese (FG) (page 13), Make 34 units with the above pieces.

SASHING UNITS FOR STORM AT SEA ROWS
FINISHED SIZE: 6″ × 12″

Make 8.

Cutting

Cut 8 background squares 6½″ × 6½″.

Assembly

1. Sew an FG unit to the top and bottom of a background square 6½″ × 6½″. Press the seam allowances toward the square. *fig. H*

2. Arrange 3 Storm at Sea blocks and 2 sashing units as shown.

3. Sew together and press the seam allowances toward the sashing unit. Make 2 rows as shown and 2 rows for the top and bottom rows that have 3 background triangles on the outer corner blocks as shown in the photo (page 44). *fig. I*

Sashing Units for Sashing Rows

Make 9.

CUTTING

Cut 9 cream squares 6½˝ × 6½˝.

ASSEMBLY

1. Sew an FG unit to each side of a background square 6½˝ × 6½˝. Press the seam allowances toward the cream square.

2. Arrange 2 panel images 6½˝ × 6½˝ and 3 sashing units as shown. Sew together and press the seam allowances toward the panels. Make 3. *fig. J*

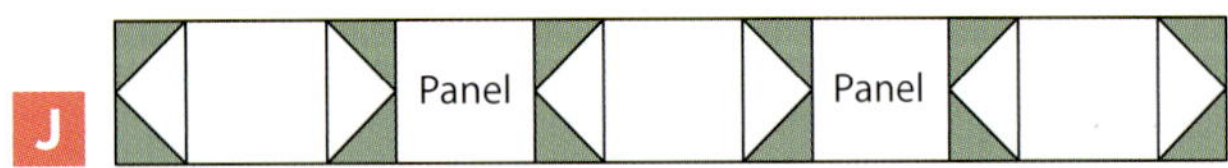

NOTE The illusion of the Sawtooth Star blocks is achieved by using a panel image in the row that appears to be the center of a Sawtooth Star block.

Inner Border

CUTTING

Cut 2 green floral strips 2˝ × WOF in half.

ASSEMBLY

1. Sew a green floral strip 2˝ × WOF to a green floral strip 2˝ × 20˝. Make 2. Press and trim strip to 2˝ × 48½˝.

2. Sew the green floral strips 2˝ × 48½˝ to the top and bottom of the quilt. Press the seam allowance toward the border.

3. Sew 2 green floral strips 2˝ × WOF together on the short edge. Make 2. Press and trim strips to 2˝ × 69½˝.

4. Sew the green floral strips 2˝ × 69½˝ to the left and right sides of the quilt. Press the seam allowance toward the border.

Outer Border

CUTTING

Cut 28 green text squares 4˝ × 4˝.

Cut 56 cream squares 3⅝˝ × 3⅝˝; subcut each square once on the diagonal.

Cut 8 medium pink, 7 soft pink, 7 medium blue, 7 light blue, 6 mint green, and 5 green floral squares 2⅝˝ × 2⅝˝.

Cut 80 background squares 2⅞˝ × 2⅞˝; subcut each square once on the diagonal.

Cut 28 background rectangles 1½˝ × 3½˝.

Cut 8 background rectangles 1½˝ × 6½˝.

Cut 12 background rectangles 1½˝ × 9½˝.

ASSEMBLY

Press all seam allowances open unless otherwise noted.

1. Sew 4 background triangles cut from 3⅝˝ × 3⅝˝ squares to a green text square 4˝ × 4˝. Press the seam allowance toward the triangles. Trim to 5½˝ × 5½˝. Make 28. *fig. K*

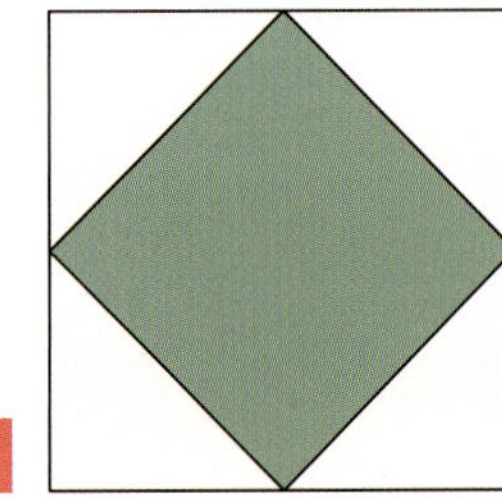

2. Sew 4 background triangles cut from 2⅞˝ × 2⅞˝ squares to each of the colored squares 2⅝˝ × 2⅝˝. Press the seam allowance toward the triangles. Trim to 3½˝ × 3½˝. Make 40.

3. Sew 3 small color Square in a Square units 3½˝ × 3½˝ in a row. Press. Make 6. *fig. L*

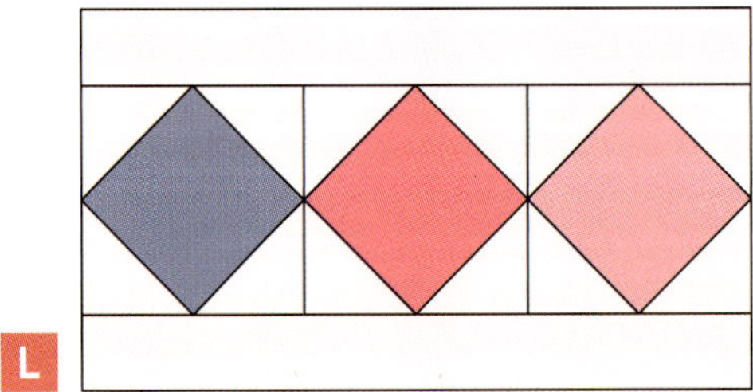

4. Sew a background rectangle 1½˝ × 9½˝ to the top and bottom of each Step 3 unit. Press the seam allowance toward the rectangles. Set aside.

5. Sew 2 small color Square in a Square units 3½˝ × 3½˝ together. Press. Make 4.

6. Sew a background rectangle 1½˝ × 6½˝ to the top and bottom of each Step 5 unit. Press the seam allowance toward the rectangles. Set aside. *fig. M*

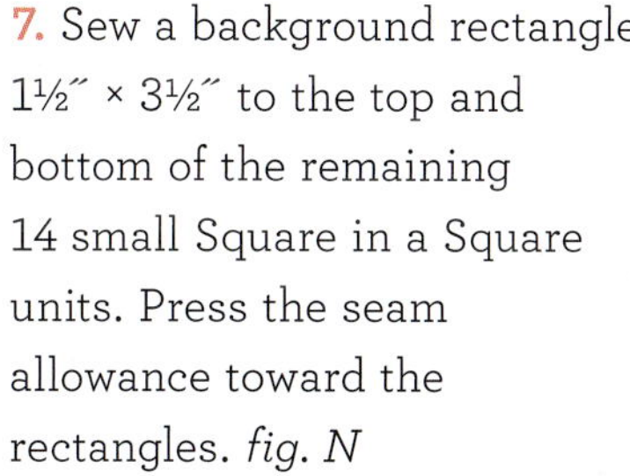

7. Sew a background rectangle 1½˝ × 3½˝ to the top and bottom of the remaining 14 small Square in a Square units. Press the seam allowance toward the rectangles. *fig. N*

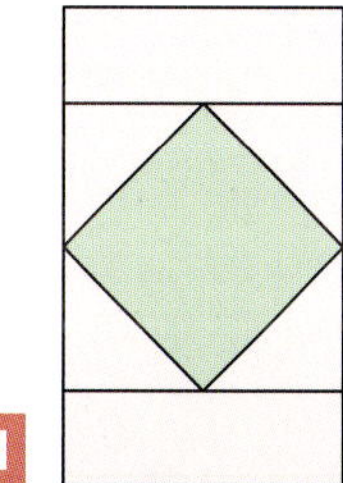

8. Lay out the top and bottom borders as illustrated, placing the colors in a pleasing fashion. Sew together and press. *fig. O*

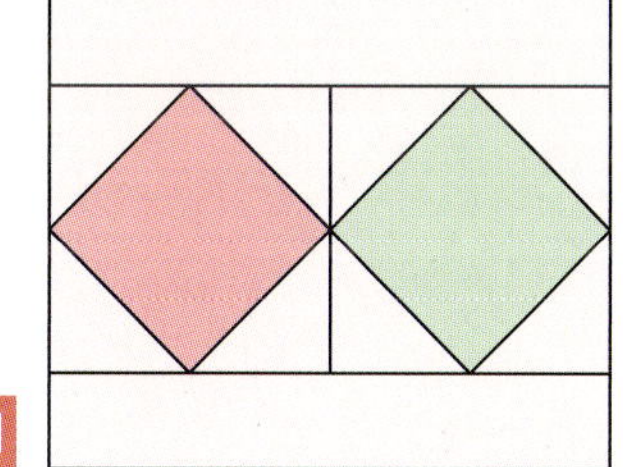

9. Lay out the left and right borders as illustrated, placing the colors in a pleasing fashion. Sew together and press. *fig. P*

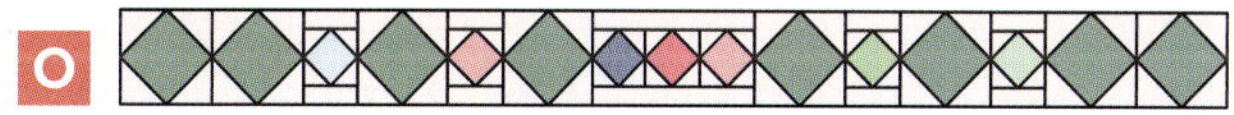

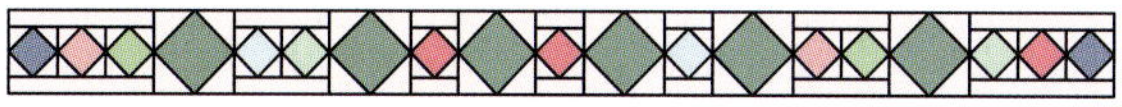

10. Sew the side borders to the quilt and press toward the inner border.

11. Sew the top and bottom borders to the quilt and press toward the inner border.

FINISHING

Layer, quilt, and bind as desired.

<h1 style="text-align:center">Make It Your Own</h1>

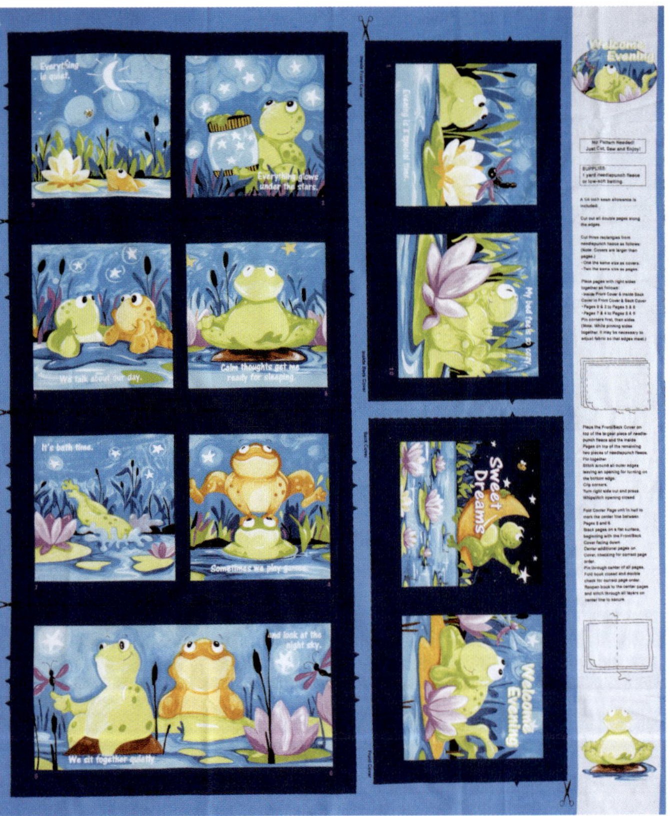

Adam Holladay created a unique version of this pattern by changing the FG units and the borders as well as swapping out some of the background squares in the sashing for colored squares. His quilt *Splish Splash* was created from a panel that was designed as a fabric book and coordinates from Clothworks!

Paul's Pond was a panel designed to sew into a fabric book.

Hip to Be Square

Design Suggestions

This pattern uses 8″ finished blocks featuring 4″ square panel images, but it is easy to adapt to panel images of almost any size. Refer to the chart at the end of the instructions to see how easy it is! Kathryn Oliphant created *Guitar Passion* (page 55) featuring the *Rock n Roll Fantasy* panel and colorful coordinates from QT Fabrics. Jump to the end to see what else she did to increase the size!

Grab a palette of your 10 favorite colors and a uniform-image-size multi-image panel to create this happy, colorful quilt. This is a perfect project for a confident beginner and goes together quickly, with the option to make it in a variety of sizes.

Materials

Yardages are based on 41˝-wide fabric.

Panel: Multi-image panel featuring 30 uniform-size images adjustable to 4½˝ × 4½˝. I used *Garden Cats* by Benartex. If you are using different size panel images, be sure to refer to the chart at the end of the instructions before cutting!

White for background: 2½ yards

Yellow: ½ yard

Royal blue: ½ yard

Light orange: ½ yard

Dark orange: ½ yard

Lime: ½ yard

Green: ½ yard

Red: ½ yard

Pink: ½ yard

Light turquoise: ½ yard

Blue: ½ yard

Binding: 1 strip 2½˝ wide from each color

Backing: 3¼ yards

Batting: 56˝ × 64˝ (twin)

Cutting

Background

Cut 6 strips 3½˝ × WOF (width of fabric).

Cut 41 strips 1½˝ × WOF.

Yellow, Royal Blue, Light Orange, Dark Orange, Lime, Green, Red, Pink, Light Turquoise, Blue

From each:

Cut 1 strip 3½˝ × WOF.

Cut 1 strip 2½˝ × WOF for binding. (You will need 6 strips × WOF or, if you want to use all 10 colors, 10 strips 2½˝ × 24˝.)

Cut 3 strips 1½˝ × WOF.

CONSTRUCTION

Before beginning any project, read the General Instructions (page 7). The construction techniques for Strip Sets (page 13) and Half-Square Triangles (HSTs) (page 11) are used in this project.

NOTE The blocks in this quilt are adapted from a traditional Jacob's Ladder Variation block. I replaced the four HSTs in the center with the panel image.

Panel Images

Adjust 30 panel images to 4½˝ × 4½˝. See Panel Preparation (page 7) for how to adjust the panel images to this size.

Half-Square Triangles

Make 12 in each of 10 colors.

CUTTING

Cut 6 color squares 3½˝ × 3½˝ from a strip 3½˝ × WOF of each of 10 colors.

Subcut 60 squares 3½˝ × 3½˝ from the background strips 3½˝ × WOF.

ASSEMBLY

Pair a color square 3½˝ × 3½˝ with a background square 3½˝ × 3½˝ to make 2 HSTs. Press and trim to 2½˝ × 2½˝. Make 12 HSTs in each color: 2 HSTs of 2 colors per block.

Four-Patch Units

Make 24 Four-Patch units of each color.

ASSEMBLY

1. Sew a color strip 1½˝ × WOF to a background strip 1½˝ × WOF. Press the seam allowance toward the color strip. Create 3 strip sets of each color.

2. Subcut 2 strip sets into rectangles 1½˝ × 2½˝ for a total of 48 rectangles of each color. Set aside the remainder of the strip sets for the Pieced Borders (below, right).

3. Using 2 subcut units, rotate 1 unit 180°. Nest the seams and stitch the units together

along the 2½˝ side to create 24 Four-Patch blocks of each color. *fig. A*

Block and Row Assembly

Press all seam allowances open unless otherwise noted.

Each block consists of a panel square plus 4 Four-Patch units and 2 HSTs of 2 colors. Make 30.

1. Lay out each block as illustrated, choosing colors in pairs for each block. *fig. B*

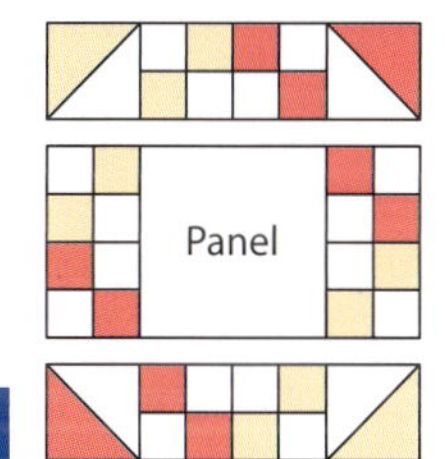

2. Stitch the pairs of Four-Patch units together.

3. Stitch 2 Four-Patch units to each side of the panel to create the center row of the block. Press the seam allowances toward the panel square. *fig. C*

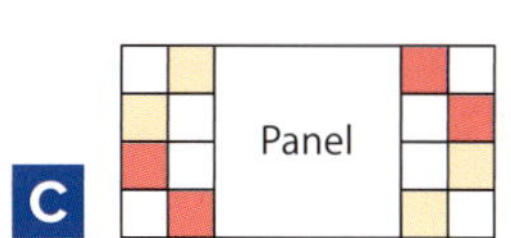

4. Sew an HST to each side of 2 pairs of Four-Patch blocks. Make 2. *fig. D*

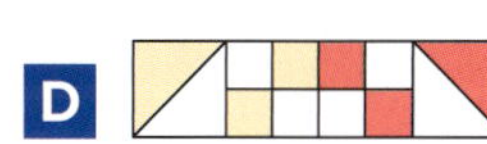

5. Sew the rows from Step 4 to the top and bottom of the row from Step 3. Block is 8½˝ × 8½˝.

6. Construct a row of 5 blocks for the body of the quilt. *fig. E*

7. Make 6 rows, placing the colors in a pleasing fashion.

Inner Borders

1. Trim 2 strips of background fabric, 1½˝ × WOF to 1½˝ × 40½˝. Sew these inner borders to the top and bottom of the quilt top. Press the seam allowance toward the border.

2. Cut a strip of background fabric 1½˝ × WOF in half to create 2 strips 1½˝ × 20½˝. Sew each of these strips to a background strip 1½˝ × WOF. Trim these 2 pieced strips to make 2 inner borders 1½˝ × 50½˝. Sew these borders to the left and right sides of the quilt top. Press the seam allowance toward the border.

Pieced Border Assembly

1. Subcut the remaining strip sets sewn in Step 1 of Four-Patch units assembly (above, left) into 1½˝ × 2½˝ units. Pair 2 units of the same color to create 96 Four-Patch blocks. *fig. F*

2. Piece 21 Four-Patch units, mixing colors as desired, for each of the top and bottom borders. Sew the top and bottom borders to the quilt. Press the seam allowance toward the background border. *fig. G*

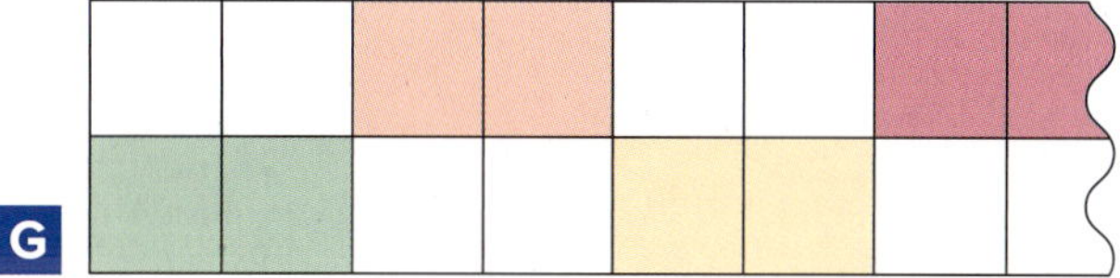

3. Piece 27 Four-Patch units, mixing colors as desired, for each of the side borders. Sew the side borders to the quilt. Press the seam allowance toward the background border.

Outer Borders Assembly

1. Cut 2 of the background strips 1½″ × WOF in half to create 4 background strips 1½″ × 20½″. Sew the background strips 1½″ × 20½″ to 4 background strips 1½″ × 40½″.

2. Trim 2 strips 1½″ × 46½″. Sew to the top and bottom of the quilt top. Press the seam allowance toward the background border.

3. Trim 2 strips 1½″ × 56½″. Sew to the left and right sides of the quilt top. Press the seam allowance toward the background border.

FINISHING

1. Quilt, bind, and add a hanging sleeve, if desired.

2. Enjoy!

Make It Your Own!

Guitar Passion Quilt by Kathryn Oliphant

Kathryn wanted to maintain the colorful border around each guitar, and this desire resulted in the panel images finishing at 7″ × 7″, so she had to adjust the math to create a larger block. Kathryn also added sashing (3½″ × 14″) and Square in a Square cornerstones (3½″ × 3½″), resulting in a much larger quilt using fewer panel images!

Kathryn chose the *Rock n Roll Fantasy Guitar Picture Patches* panel and coordinates from QT Fabrics.

Chart for Alternate-Size Panel Images

Panel image: cutsize	Panel image: finished size	Squares for HSTs: cut size	HSTs: finished size	Four-patch strips: cut size	Four-patch: finished size
5½″ × 5½″	5″ × 5″	3½″ × 3½″	2½″ × 2½″	1¾″ × WOF	2½″ × 2½″
6½″ × 6½″	6″ × 6″	4″ × 4″	3″ × 3″	2″ × WOF	3″ × 3″
7½″ × 7½″	7″ × 7″	4½″ × 4½″	3½″ × 3½″	2¼″ × WOF	3½″ × 3½″
8½″ × 8½″	8″ × 8″	5″ × 5″	4″ × 4″	2½″ × WOF	4″ × 4″

When Night Falls, the Forest Sings

Design Suggestions

I used the *Rainforest Glow* panel and solid coordinates from Benartex. Mixing the color combinations in the stars and placing the panel images in the center section of the Dutch Rose quilt block created a fun way to highlight the individual images. A variety of stars in the borders added to the impression of a night sky. This quilt could easily be adapted to accommodate larger or fewer panel images. See Margaret Matchett's *Averi's Butterfly Dreams*, adapted from this project (page 65).

A galaxy of colorful stars is sprinkled across this quilt, which features rainforest frogs. Learn how to do partial seams in the border construction, and you'll discover they are easier than you might think!

Materials

Yardages are based on 41˝-wide fabrics.

Panel: Multiple-image panel featuring uniform-size images adjustable to 6˝ × 6˝. I used the *Rainforest Glow* panel from Benartex.

Indigo blue for background: 4¾ yards

Green: ⅝ yard

Red: ⅝ yard

Orange: ⅝ yard

Yellow: ⅝ yard

Light blue: ⅝ yard

Dark blue: ⅝ yard

Polka dot: 1 yard for blocks and binding

Backing: 5 yards

Batting: 71˝ × 86˝

Cutting

All rectangles and squares for the individual blocks will be subcut from the following strips.

Indigo Blue

Cut 1 strip 8˝ × WOF (width of fabric).

Cut 2 strips 7¼˝ × WOF.

Cut 8 strips 6½˝ × WOF.

Cut 12 strips 3½˝ × WOF for Flying Geese (FG) rectangles (subcut as listed below).

Cut 4 strips 3˝ × WOF.

Cut 2 strips 2½˝ × WOF.

Cut 14 strips 2˝ × WOF.

Green, Red, Orange, Yellow, and Dark Blue

From each:

Cut 1 strip 3˝ × WOF.

Cut 3 strips 2½˝ × WOF.

Cut 3 strips 2˝ × WOF.

Light Blue

Cut 2 strips 3˝ × WOF.

Cut 3 strips 2½˝ × WOF.

Cut 3 strips 2˝ × WOF.

Polka Dot

Cut 2 strips 3˝ × WOF.

Cut 8 strips 2½˝ × WOF for binding.

CONSTRUCTION

Before beginning any project, read the General Instructions (page 7). This project uses construction techniques for Half-Square Triangles (HSTs) (page 11) and Flying Geese (FG) units (page 13).

Panel Images

Adjust 14 panel images to 6½˝ × 6½˝. See Panel Preparation (page 7) for how to adjust the panel images to this size.

Dutch Rose Block

FINISHED BLOCK: 12˝ × 12˝

Make 14.

I made 14 stars, using the following 2-color combinations:

- Yellow and dark blue
- Orange and green
- Red and green
- Orange and dark blue
- Yellow and light blue
- Dark blue and green
- Yellow and red
- Orange and light blue
- Red and dark blue
- Yellow and green
- Red and orange
- Light blue and green
- Red and light blue
- Yellow and orange

CUTTING

For each star, subcut pieces from the strips above as follows, substituting the 2 colors you select.

Cut 6 red squares 2½˝ × 2½˝.

Cut 12 red squares 2˝ × 2˝.

Cut 6 yellow squares 2½˝ × 2½˝.

Cut 12 yellow squares 2˝ × 2˝.

Cut 16 indigo blue rectangles 2˝ × 3½˝ (subcut from 3½˝ × WOF strips).

Cut 4 indigo blue squares 2˝ × 2˝.

ASSEMBLY

Press all seam allowances open unless otherwise noted.

1. Sew a red square 2˝ × 2˝ to the right end and a yellow square 2˝ × 2˝ to the left end of an indigo blue rectangle 2˝ × 3½˝ to make an FG unit. Make 12. *fig. A*

2. Sew 2 FG units together. Make 2. Press. *fig. B*

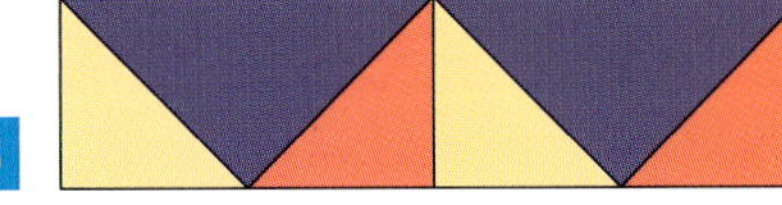

3. Pair a red square 2½˝ × 2½˝ with a yellow square 2½˝ × 2½˝ and sew 2 HSTs. Press and trim to 2˝ × 2˝. Make 8 HSTs.

4. Sew a HST to each end of a single FG unit. Color placement is key! Press. Make 2. *fig. C*

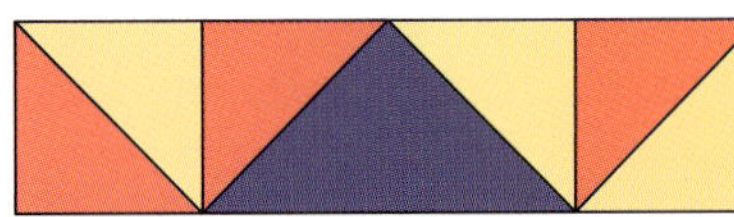

5. Sew the unit from Step 2 to the top of the unit from Step 4. Press. Make 2. *fig. D*

6. Sew the units from Step 5 to the left and right sides of your panel image. Press the seam allowance toward the panel image. *fig. E*

7. Arrange 2 indigo blue rectangles 2˝ × 3½˝ and 2 FG as shown. Sew together and press the center seam allowances open and the outer seam allowances toward the rectangles. Make 2. *fig. F*

8. Arrange 4 HSTs, an FG, and 2 indigo blue squares 2˝ × 2˝ as shown. Pay close attention to the orientation of the HST. Sew together and press the inner seam allowances open and the outer seam allowances toward the squares. Make 2. *fig. G*

9. Sew the unit from Step 7 to the top of the row from Step 8. Press. Make 2. *fig. H*

10. Sew these rows to the top and bottom of the Step 6 panel image to complete the block. Press the seam allowances toward the panel image.

NOTE This block is a variation of a traditional Dutch Rose block. I chose to create space for the panel image by eliminating the Sawtooth Star from the center of the block and using the framework around that portion of the block to highlight the panel image. I also altered the color placement from the original block.

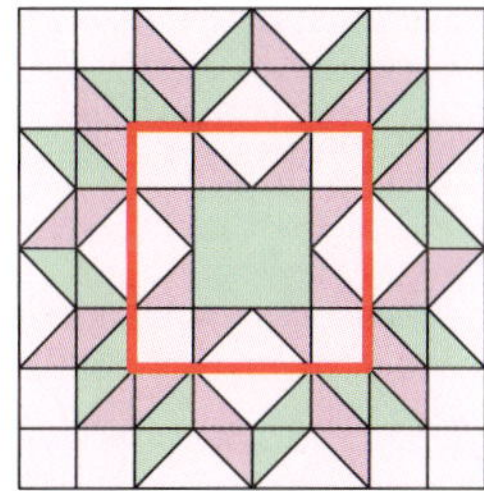

Lemoyne Star

FINISHED SIZE: 6˝ × 6˝

Make 6.

I made 6 stars, using the following 2-color combinations:

- Dark blue and green
- Red and orange
- Light blue and red
- Yellow and orange
- Dark blue and yellow
- Orange and green

CUTTING

Cut 4 green squares 2½˝ × 2½˝.

Cut 4 dark blue squares 2½˝ × 2½˝.

Cut 4 indigo blue squares 2½˝ × 2½˝.

Cut 4 indigo blue squares 2˝ × 2˝.

ASSEMBLY

Press all seam allowances open unless otherwise noted.

1. Pair a green square 2½˝ × 2½˝ with a dark blue square 2½˝ × 2½˝ to make 2 HSTs. Press and trim to 2˝ × 2˝. Make 4 HSTs.

2. Pair a green square 2½˝ × 2½˝ with an indigo blue square 2½˝ × 2½˝ to make 2 HSTs. Press and trim to 2˝ × 2˝. Make 4 HSTs.

3. Pair a dark blue square 2½˝ × 2½˝ with an indigo blue square 2½˝ × 2½˝ to make 2 HSTs. Press and trim to 2˝ × 2˝. Make 4 HSTs.

4. Lay out the HSTs and indigo blue squares 2˝ × 2˝ as illustrated, sew together each of the 4 rows, and press. *fig. I*

5. Sew the rows together and press.

6. Repeat Steps 1–5 to sew the 5 remaining Lemoyne Star blocks.

Spotlight Stars

FINISHED SIZE: 4½˝ × 4½˝

Make 14.

CUTTING

Cut the following star pieces from the 3˝ × WOF strips. Use the Spotlight Star and Spotlight Side templates (page 124).

Green, red, orange: 2 blocks each

Yellow: 1 block

Light blue: 3 blocks

Polka dot: 4 blocks

For each block:

Cut 4 star points with the Spotlight Star template.

Cut 4 indigo blue pairs (left and right) with the Spotlight Side template.

Press all seam allowances open unless otherwise noted.

1. Sew a side triangle to the right side of the star point. Press the seam allowance toward the side triangle. *fig. A*

2. Sew a side triangle to the left side of the star point. Press the seam allowance toward the side triangle. *fig. B*

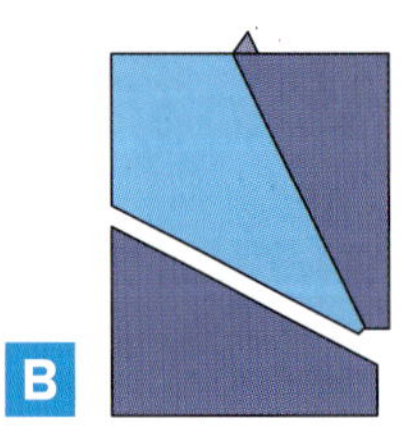

3. Trim the unit to 2¾˝ × 2¾˝, being sure to line up the ruler with the diagonal line going from the tip to the corner of the unit. Trim the corner with the slim point first. *fig. C*

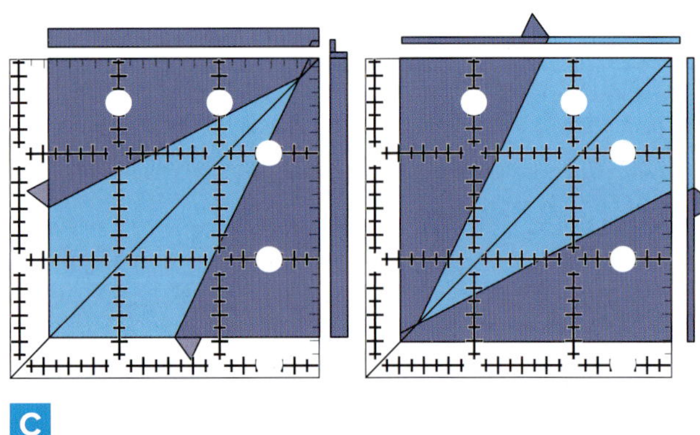

4. Sew each pair of units together and then sew the rows together to create the Spotlight Star block. Press. *fig. D*

5. Repeat Steps 1–4 to make 14 Spotlight Star blocks.

Upper-Left/Lower-Right Corner Blocks

FINISHED SIZE: 13½˝ × 18˝

Make 2.

CUTTING

Cut the pieces below from the 6½˝ × WOF and the 8˝ × WOF indigo blue strips cut previously.

Cut 2 indigo blue rectangles 8˝ × 11˝.

Cut 2 indigo blue rectangles 8˝ × 6½˝.

Cut 2 indigo blue rectangles 8˝ × 2˝.

Cut 2 indigo blue rectangles 6½˝ × 5˝.

Cut 2 indigo blue rectangles 6½˝ × 2˝.

Assembly

Press all seam allowances open unless otherwise noted.

Select 2 Lemoyne Stars for the upper-left and 2 Lemoyne Stars for the lower-right corner blocks.

1. Sew an indigo blue rectangle 6½˝ × 2˝ to one side of a star. Press the seam allowance toward the rectangle. *fig. E*

2. Sew an indigo blue rectangle 8˝ × 2˝ to an adjacent side of the star in Step 1. Press the seam allowance toward the rectangle. *fig. F*

3. Sew the indigo blue rectangle 8˝ × 11˝ to the bottom of the star from Step 2. Press the seam allowance toward the rectangle. Set aside. *fig. G*

F

G

4. Sew an indigo blue rectangle 6½˝ × 5˝ to the top of the second Lemoyne Star 6˝ × 6˝. Press the seam allowance toward the rectangle. *fig. H*

5. Sew an indigo blue rectangle 6½˝ × 8˝ to the bottom of this star. Press the seam allowance toward the rectangle. *fig. I*

H

I

6. Sew the Step 3 and 5 units together to create the upper-left corner block. Press.

7. Repeat Steps 1–6 to make the lower-right corner block, rotating the finished block 180°.

Upper-Right/Lower-Left Corner Blocks

FINISHED SIZE: 7½˝ × 12˝

Make 2.

CUTTING

Subcut from indigo blue strip 6½˝ × WOF cut previously.

Cut 2 indigo blue rectangles 6½˝ × 2˝.

Cut 2 indigo blue rectangles 6½˝ × 5˝.

Subcut from indigo blue strip 2˝ × WOF cut previously.

Cut 2 indigo blue rectangles 2˝ × 12½˝.

ASSEMBLY

Press all seam allowances open unless otherwise noted.

Select a Lemoyne Star 6˝ × 6˝ for the upper-right corner block and another Lemoyne Star for the lower-left corner block.

1. Sew an indigo blue rectangle 6½˝ × 2˝ to the top of a Lemoyne Star. Press the seam allowance toward the rectangle. *fig. J*

2. Sew an indigo blue rectangle 6½˝ × 5˝ to the bottom of the Step 1 star unit. Press the seam allowance toward the rectangle. *fig. K*

J

K

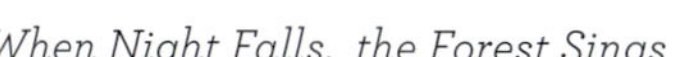

3. Sew an indigo blue rectangle 2˝ × 12½˝ to the right side of the Step 2 star unit. Press the seam allowance toward the rectangle. Make 2 and rotate the block 180° for the lower-left corner block. *fig. L*

4. Rotate the block 180° for the upper-right corner block.

Rows and Sashing

CUTTING

Cut 4 indigo blue rectangles 7¼˝ × 12½˝.

Cut 4 indigo blue rectangles 6½˝ × 12½˝.

Cut 9 indigo blue strips 2˝ × 12½˝.

ASSEMBLY

Row 1 and Row 5

1. Arrange an indigo blue sashing strip 2˝ × 12½˝, 2 Dutch Rose blocks, and 2 indigo blue rectangles 6½˝ × 12½˝ as shown. Sew together and press the seam allowances away from the blocks. Make 2. *fig. M*

2. Sew the upper-right corner block to the right end of a Step 1 unit. Press the seam allowance toward the corner block. This is Row 1. *fig. N*

3. Sew the lower-left corner block to the left end of a Step 1 unit. Press the seam allowance toward the corner block. This is Row 5. *fig. O*

Row 2 and Row 4

Arrange 2 indigo blue sashing strips, 3 Dutch Rose blocks, and an indigo blue rectangle 7¼˝ × 12½˝ as shown. Sew together and press the inner seam allowances toward the sashing strips and the outer seam allowances toward the rectangles. *fig. P*

Row 3

1. Sew an indigo blue sashing strip 2˝ × 12½˝ between each of 4 Dutch Rose blocks. Press the seam allowance toward the sashing strips. *fig. Q*

2. Sew 6 indigo blue 2˝ × WOF strips together end to end. Subcut into 4 strips 2˝ × 53˝.

3. Sew an indigo blue sashing strip 2˝ × 53˝ to the top of Row 2 and the bottom of Row 4. Press the seam allowance toward the strip.

4. Sew an indigo blue sashing strip 2˝ × 53˝ to the top and bottom of Row 3. Press the seam allowance toward the sashing strip.

5. Sew Rows 2–4 together. Press the seam allowances toward the sashing strips. *fig. R*

R

Borders

CUTTING

Cut 14 indigo blue strips 2˝ × 5˝.

Cut 2 indigo blue strips 6½˝ × 2˝.

Cut 2 indigo blue strips 6½˝ × 33½˝.

Cut 2 indigo blue strips 6½˝ × 41˝.

ASSEMBLY

Press all seam allowances open unless otherwise noted.

Top and Bottom Rows and Borders

1. Sew an indigo blue strip 2˝ × 5˝ to a side of each of the 14 Spotlight Stars. Press the seam allowance toward the strip. *fig. A*

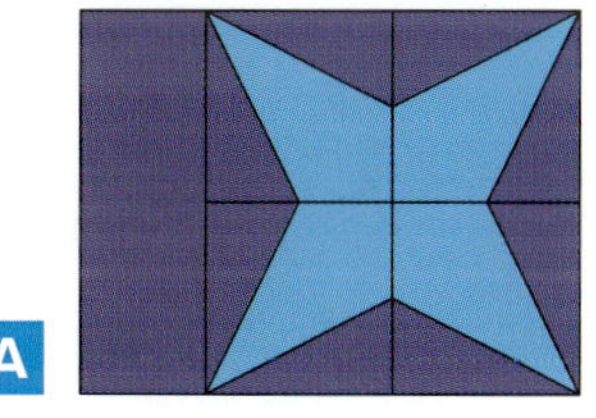

A

2. Select 3 Spotlight Stars and sew together, alternating the orientation of the strip, with the first star's strip at the top, the second at the bottom, and the third at the top. Make 2 sets. Press. *fig. B*

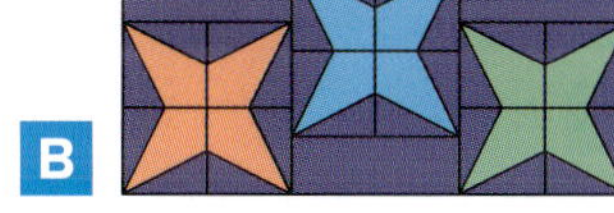

B

3. Sew an indigo blue strip 6½˝ × 32˝ to the end of the row of 3 stars. Make 2. Press the seam allowance toward the long strip. *fig. C*

C 

4. Align a border strip from Step 3 to the top of Row 1, placing the Spotlight Stars on the right end. Align the other Step 3 border strip with the bottom of Row 5 and with the Spotlight Stars on the left end. Sew together and press the seam allowance toward the border strip. *fig. D*

D

5. Sew the upper-left corner block to the left end of Row 1. Press the seam allowance toward the upper-left corner block.

6. Sew the lower-right corner block to the right end of Row 5. Press the seam allowance toward the lower-right corner block.

7. Align Row 1 with the right end of Row 2, matching the seam allowance in the upper-left corner block to the left edge of Row 2. Sew together with a partial seam allowance, stopping about 4˝ from the end of Row 2. Row 1 will extend beyond Row 2.

8. Align Row 5 with the left end of Row 4, matching the seam allowance in the lower-right corner block to the right edge of Row 4. Sew together with a partial seam allowance, stopping about 4˝ from the end of Row 4. Row 5 will extend beyond Row 4. *fig. E*

Side Borders

1. Sew an indigo blue strip 2˝ × 6½˝ to a side of 2 Spotlight Stars. Press the seam allowance toward the strip. These stars are the first stars in the side borders. *fig. F*

2. Select 3 Spotlight Stars and sew together, alternating the orientation of the strip with the first star's strip to the bottom, the second to the top and the third to the bottom. Press. Make 2. *fig. G*

3. Sew a star from Step 1 to the left end of a row of 3 stars, with the 2˝ strips on the top and left of the row. Press. Make 2. *fig. H*

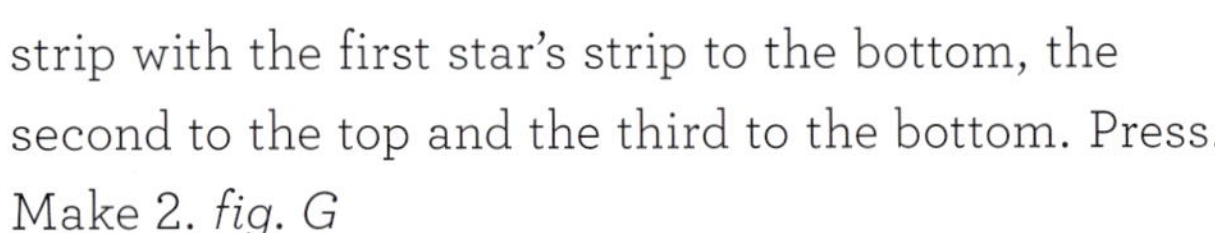

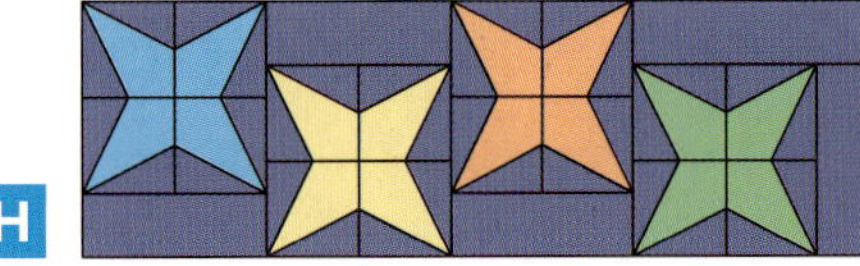

4. Sew an indigo blue strip 6½˝ × 41˝ to the last star in each row of the Step 3 units. Press the seam allowances toward the strip. *fig. I*

5. Sew a border with stars at the bottom to the left side of the quilt, aligning the lower corner and the top of the sashing on Row 2. Press the seam allowance toward the border.

6. Sew a border with stars at the top to the right side of the quilt, aligning the upper corner and the bottom of the sashing on Row 4. Press the seam allowance toward the border.

7. Sew the rest of the seam of Row 1, completing the partial seam. Press the seam allowance toward the sashing on Row 2.

8. Sew the rest of Row 5, completing the partial seam. Press the seam allowance toward the sashing on Row 4. *fig. J*

Quilt assembly

FINISHING

1. Quilt, bind, and add a hanging sleeve, as desired.

2. Enjoy!

Make It Your Own!

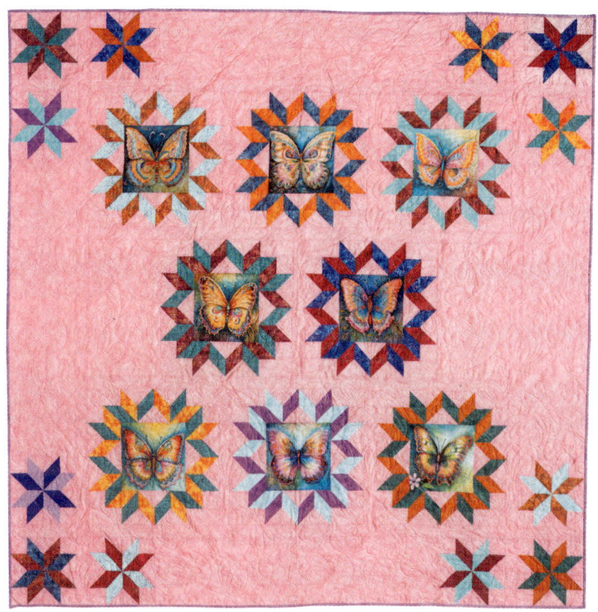

Averi's Butterfly Dreams by Margaret Matchett

Margaret chose the *Spring Bling* panel from QT Fabrics.

Margaret Matchett chose a panel with 8˝ × 8˝ images and decided to use fewer blocks to create this quilt for her granddaughter. Because she had to increase the size of the blocks, she also chose to keep the border fairly simple by eliminating some of the motifs and the partial seam from the original instructions. See below for a chart on how to use different-size panel images.

Chart for Alternate-Size Panel Images

Panel image: cut size	Panel image: finished size	Squares for HSTs: cut size	Squares including FG square: cut size	Finished HSTs and squares	FG rectangles: cut size	Finished FG
7½˝ × 7½˝	7˝ × 7˝	2¾˝ × 2¾˝	2¼˝ × 2¼˝	1¾˝ × 1¾˝	2¼˝ × 4˝	1¾˝ × 3½˝
8½˝ × 8½˝	8˝ × 8˝	3˝ × 3˝	2½˝ × 2½˝	2˝ × 2˝	2½˝ × 4½˝	2˝ × 4˝

Spooky Table Runner

FINISHED RUNNER: 45″ × 21″

Design Suggestions

In this runner, the possibilities are limited only by your imagination. You might choose to make a longer runner with 4 blocks and panel images or perhaps use only 2 panel images with a patchwork center block, as Susan Wiley did in *Sewing and Sowing My Garden* (page 71).

Dress up your holiday table for a festive event! Pair a coordinating table runner with a set of place mats for an extra special gift or table setting. I used the All Hallows Eve *panel and coordinates by Benartex and featured the panel images in 2 different blocks.*

Materials

Yardages are based on 41˝-wide fabrics.

Panel: Multi-image panel with uniform-size images adjustable to 6½˝ × 6½˝. I used the *All Hallows Eve* panel from Benartex.

Black: ⅜ yard

Purple: ½ yard

Yellow: ⅜ yard

White: ⅛ yard

Orange: ½ yard

Blue swirl: ⅜ yard

Medium blue: ¼ yard

Green: ¼ yard

Binding: ⅜ yard

Backing: 1½ yards

Batting: 25˝ × 49˝

Cutting

Subcut all squares and rectangles from the following pieces.

Black

Cut 3 strips 2½˝ × WOF (width of fabric).

Purple

Cut 1 strip 4˝ × WOF.

Cut 1 strip 3½˝ × WOF.

Cut 3 strips 2½˝ × WOF.

Yellow

Cut 1 strip 3½˝ × WOF.

Cut 1 strip 2½˝ × WOF.

Cut 2 strips 1¼˝ × WOF.

White

Cut 2 strips 1¼˝ × WOF.

Orange

Cut 1 strip 4˝ × WOF.

Cut 1 strip 3½˝ × WOF.

Cut 1 strip 2½˝ × WOF.

Cut 2 strips 2˝ × WOF.

Cut 1 strip 1½˝ × WOF.

Blue Swirl

Cut 2 strips 3½˝ × WOF.

Medium Blue

Cut 3 strips 2˝ × WOF.

Green

Cut 1 strip 3½˝ × WOF.

Cut 1 strip 1½˝ × WOF.

Binding

Cut 4 strips 2½˝ × WOF.

CONSTRUCTION

Before beginning any project, read the General Instructions (page 7). This project uses construction techniques for Strip Sets (page 13), Half-Square Triangles (HSTs) (page 11), Pinwheels (page 12), and Flying Geese (FG) units (page 13).

Panel Images

FINISHED PANEL IMAGE: 6˝ × 6˝

Trim all panel images to 6½˝ × 6½˝. If needed, add coping strips around your panel images to bring them up to this size.

Pinwheels

FINISHED BLOCK: 3˝ × 3˝

CUTTING

Cut 40 black squares 2½˝ × 2½˝.

Cut 40 purple squares 2½˝ × 2½˝.

ASSEMBLY

1. Pair a black square 2½˝ × 2½˝ with a purple square 2½˝ × 2½˝ to make 2 HSTs. Make a total of 80 black and purple HSTs. Press and trim to 2˝ × 2˝.

2. Sew 4 HSTs together to make 20 pinwheels. *fig. A*

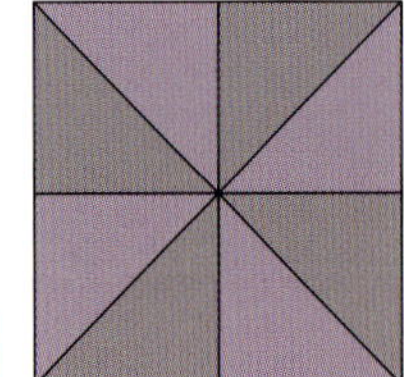

Candy Corn

FINISHED BLOCK: 3˝ × 3˝

CUTTING

From the blue swirl 3½˝ × WOF strip, cut 20 pairs of background triangles by using the Candy Corn Background template (page 124) or a Tri-Recs tool. Be sure you have 20 left and 20 right triangles, which is achieved easily by cutting the shapes from your strip folded with wrong sides together.

1. Arrange a white strip 1¼˝ × WOF, an orange strip 2˝ × WOF, and a yellow strip 1¼˝ × WOF as shown. Sew together and press the seam allowances toward the yellow strip. Make 4 strip sets. *fig. B*

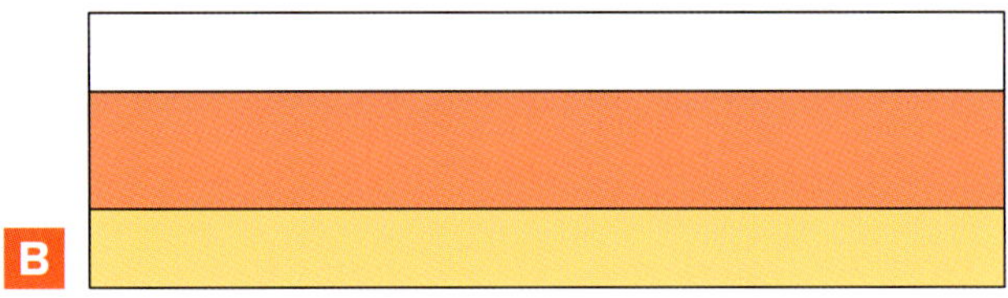

2. Using the Candy Corn template (page 124) or a Tri-Recs tool, cut 20 wedges 3½˝, keeping the yellow strip at the bottom or widest part of the triangle shape. *fig. C*

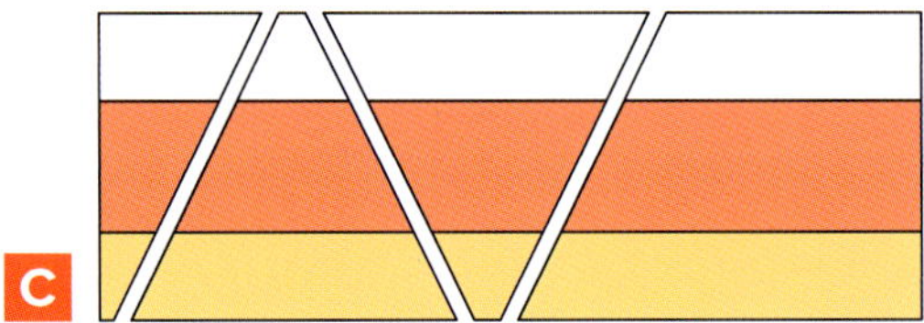

3. Sew the background triangles to each side of the Candy Corn, pressing toward the background triangle. *fig. D*

4. Set aside the Pinwheel and Candy Corn blocks until the center of the runner is constructed.

Spooky Star

FINISHED SIZE: 12˝ × 12˝

Make 2.

CUTTING

Cut the following V-block pieces from the 3½˝ × WOF strips. Use the Candy Corn and Candy Corn Background templates (page 124) or a Tri-Recs tool.

Yellow: Cut 16 wedges with the Candy Corn template.

Orange: Cut 8 pairs of background triangles by using the Candy Corn Background template.

Green: Cut 8 pairs of background triangles by using the Candy Corn Background template.

Be sure you have both a left and right background triangle for each set, which is achieved easily by cutting the shapes from your strip folded with wrong sides together.

ASSEMBLY

1. Sew 8 V-block units using a green left background triangle and an orange right background triangle and 8 V-block units using an orange left background triangle and a green right background triangle. *fig. E*

2. Sew a pair of **each** of the V-blocks together to make 8 units. *fig. F*

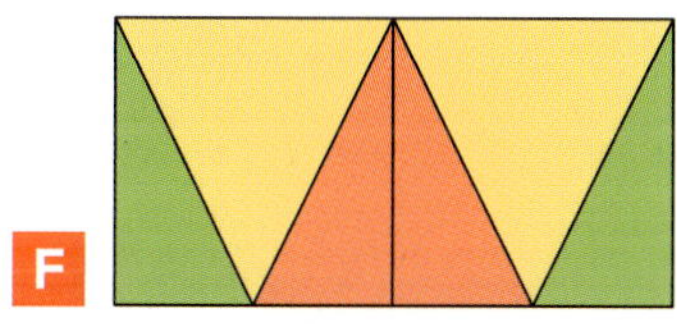

3. Sew a strip set using the yellow strip 2½″ × WOF and the orange strip 1½″ × WOF. Subcut 8 units 2½″ × 3½″. *fig. G*

4. Sew a strip set using the orange strip 2½″ × WOF and the green strip 1½″ × WOF. Subcut 8 units 1½″ × 3½″. *fig. H*

5. Sew a yellow/orange unit from Step 3 to an orange/green unit from Step 4 to create a corner unit. Make 8. *fig. I*

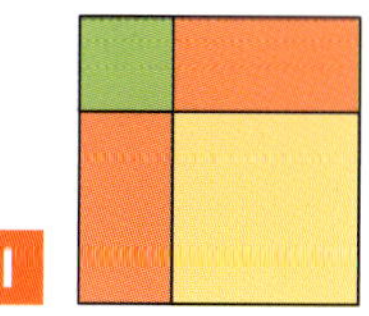

6. Sew a corner unit from Step 5 to each end of a unit sewn in Step 2, being sure to orient the corners correctly. *fig. J*

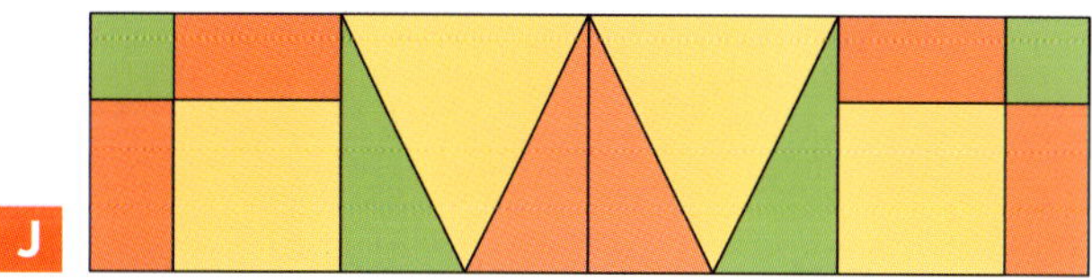

7. Arrange the units from Steps 2 and 6 with the panel square as shown. Sew the Step 2 V-block units to the sides of the panel and then sew the rows together. Press.

Weathervane Variation

FINISHED SIZE: 12″ × 12″

CUTTING

Cut 4 blue swirl squares 3½″ × 3½″.

Cut 4 green squares 3½″ × 3½″.

Weathervane

Cut 4 purple rectangles 3½″ × 6½″.

Cut 2 purple squares 4″ × 4″.

Cut 2 orange squares 4″ × 4″.

ASSEMBLY

1. Sew a blue swirl square 3½″ × 3½″ to the left end of a purple rectangle 3½″ × 6½″ and a green square 3½″ × 3½″ on the right end to create an FG unit. Make 4. *fig. K*

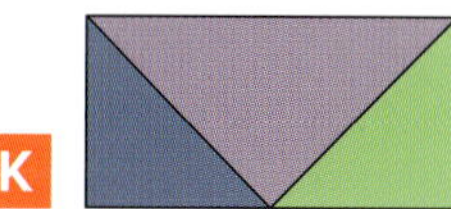

2. Pair a purple square 4″ × 4″ and an orange square 4″ × 4″ to make 2 HSTs. Sew together and cut apart. Press and trim to 3½″ × 3½″. Make 4 HSTs.

3. Sew an HST to each end of 2 FG, orienting as illustrated. *fig. L*

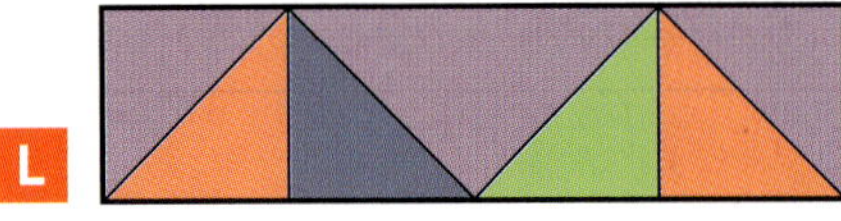

4. Arrange the units from Steps 1–2 with the panel image as shown. Sew together, being careful to orient the FG correctly. Press. *fig. M*

CUTTING FOR TABLE RUNNER BORDER

Cut 2 medium blue strips 2˝ × 36½˝.

Cut 2 medium blue strips 2˝ × 15½˝.

ASSEMBLY

Press all seam allowances open unless otherwise noted.

1. Sew a Spooky Star block to the left and right sides of the Weathervane center block. Press.

2. Sew a 2˝ × 36½˝ medium blue border strip to the top and bottom of the Step 1 row. Press the seam allowances toward the border.

3. Sew a 2˝ × 15½˝ medium blue border strip to the short ends of this row of blocks. Press the seam allowances toward the border.

4. Sew 2 Candy Corn blocks and 3 Pinwheels together and press. Make 2. Sew to the left and right ends of the runner. *fig. N*

5. Sew 8 Candy Corn blocks and 7 Pinwheel blocks together and press. Make 2. Sew to the top and bottom of the table runner. *fig. O*

FINISHING

1. Quilt and bind as desired.

2. Enjoy!

Make It Your Own!

FINISHED RUNNER: 16″ × 41″

Sewing and Sowing My Garden by Susan Wiley

Susan chose the *Love Grows Here* panel and coordinates from Benartex. This quilt was partially inspired by *Bee Mine*, designed by Mary Hertel, and *Patsy's Perfect Blooms*, designed by Dodi Lee Poulsen. Both projects are available for purchase at **QuiltingDaily.com**. The quilt was also partially inspired by various elements found in *Tablerunner Bliss* by Sherri Falls.

Because her panel had fewer panel images and the images were larger, Susan adapted the basic concept of the table-runner pattern and made it work for the panel images she had. She chose a fun center block with hearts and flowers to complement the theme of the fabric.

Trick-or-Treat Bag

FINISHED BAG: 6″ WIDE × 6¾″ TALL × 5″ DEEP

Leftover Halloween panel images can be incorporated into cute small bags for your favorite kiddos to carry for trick-or-treating—no more pillowcases or plastic shopping bags! They won't lose this one!

DESIGN SUGGESTIONS

Small bags using panel images can be used for gift bags, trick-or-treat bags, lunch bags, and anywhere your imagination takes you! Use up those smaller panel images by incorporating them into a unique and thoughtful bag that will be cherished by the receiver.

Materials

Yardages are based on 41″-wide fabrics.

Panel: 1–2 panel images adjustable to 6½″ × 6½″

Medium-weight fusible stabilizer: 3″ × 6″ (to reinforce bag bottom)

Blue for lining, handles, sides, and bottom: ¾ yard

Interfacing: 1 yard, optional

Cutting

Panel

Trim and square 1 or 2 panel images to 7″ × 7″.

Blue

Cut 2 strips 2¼″ × 9½″.

Cut 1 strip 3½″ × 7″.

Cut 2 strips 2¼″ × 15½″.

Cut 2 strips 5″ × 12″.

Cut 1 piece 8½″ × 18″.

Stabilizer

Cut 1 rectangle 3″ × 6″.

CONSTRUCTION

Construct using ½″ seam allowance.

Before beginning any project, read the General Instructions (page 7). How to square up larger panel images is addressed in Squaring Up Panel Images (page 7).

If you decide to use the optional stabilizer, fuse it to all cut pieces except the blue handles 5″ × 12″.

1. Sew the blue strip 3½″ × 7″ to the bottom of the front panel image. Press the seam allowance toward the blue strip.

2. Sew the bottom of the back panel image to the blue strip 3½″ × 7″. Press the seam allowance toward the blue strip. *fig. A*

3. Center the 3″ × 6″ stabilizer on the bottom blue strip and fuse. Mark the center of the bottom on each end.

4. Sew a blue strip 2¼″ × 15½″ to each side of the central panel section. Press the seam allowance toward the strips. *fig. B*

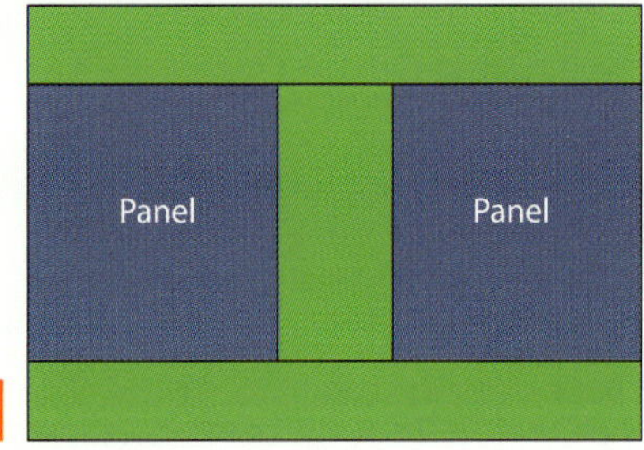

5. Sew a blue strip 2¼″ × 9½″ to the top of each panel image and press toward the panel image.

6. Fold the bag right sides together so the panel images are facing each other and sew the side seams. Backstitch at the start and finish of the seam. Press.

7. Create boxed corners by pulling the front and back of the bag away from each other to form a triangle at the bottom. Match the marked center line on the bottom with the side seam and pin.

8. Measure 2½˝ from the tip of the triangle and draw a line along the base of the triangle. Stitch on the line, being sure to backstitch at both ends. You may wish to catch the edge of the stabilizer in your stitching.

9. Cut away the triangle ½˝ from the stitching. *fig. C*

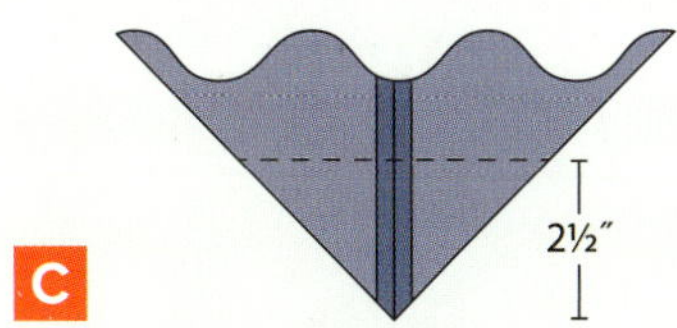

10. Turn the bag right-side out and push the corners into shape by using a point turner.

11. Fold the top edge 1˝ to the inside and press.

12. Fold the lining piece right sides together and sew each side together, backstitching at the start and finish of the seams. Press the bottom fold and press the seam allowances open.

13. Create boxed corners by following Steps 7–9. Match the side seams to the bottom crease and pin.

14. Fold the blue handle strips 5˝ × 12˝ in half lengthwise, wrong sides together, and press.

15. Open the strips and fold each half lengthwise into the center crease, wrong sides together, and press. *fig. D*

16. Fold again on the center crease and press. Stitch ⅛˝ from each folded edge to make 2 handles.

17. Mark the center of each side of the lining. Pin each end of one handle 2˝ away from the center line, matching the raw edge of the handle to the raw edge of the lining. Stitch each end of the handle to the lining by sewing a scant 1˝ square with an X through it to secure the handles to the lining.

18. Repeat for the other handle on the other side of the lining.

19. Fold the top edge of the lining 1˝ to the inside and press.

20. Turn the lining inside out and place it inside the outer bag, matching the side seams' top folded edges. Pin all the way around the bag.

21. Stitch together ¼˝ from the top edge of the bag. Stitch again ⅛˝ from the edge of the bag.

22. Push the corners of the lining into the corners of the outer bag.

23. Enjoy!

Spooky Place Mats

Design Suggestions

I designed these place mats to feature the Halloween-themed panel *All Hallows Eve* and a selection of coordinating prints and solids from Benartex. I chose 4 panel images to highlight in a variety of traditional quilt blocks, but you could certainly simply choose one and make them all the same! I added fun related motifs, such as candy corn, ribbon candy, stars, and moons. Other motifs, such as a black cat, bat, and pumpkin, would also make fun additions. Be sure to take a look at Susan Wiley's *Sewing and Sowing My Garden* place mats (page 82).

Place mats are a quick and easy way to use panel images to make wonderful gifts for all occasions! Grab a set of 4 (or more) panel images and play!

Materials

Yardages are based on 41˝-wide fabrics.

Panel: Multi-image panel with uniform-size images adjustable to 6½˝ × 6½˝. I used *All Hallows Eve* by Benartex. You'll need 4 panel images.

Yellow: ⅜ yard

Green: ⅓ yard

Blue: ⅓ yard

Dark blue: ⅓ yard

Black print: ¾ yard (also for binding)

Black: ¼ yard

Medium orange: ¼ yard

Dark orange: ⅓ yard

Purple: ⅓ yard

White: ⅛ yard

Fusible product of your choice: ½ yard, optional, for appliqués

Backing: 1½ yards

Batting: 4 pieces 16˝ × 22˝

Candy Corn B Templates (page 125) or Tri-Recs ruler (recommended)

Cutting

All squares and rectangles will be cut from the following strips.

Yellow

Cut 1 strip 3½˝ × WOF (width of fabric).

Cut 1 strip 3˝ × WOF.

Cut 1 strip 2½˝ × WOF.

Cut 2 strips 1½˝ × WOF.

Green

Cut 1 strip 3½˝ × WOF.

Cut 1 strip 3˝ × WOF.

Cut 1 strip 2˝ × WOF.

Blue

Cut 1 strip 6½˝ × WOF.

Cut 1 strip 2½˝ × WOF.

Black Print

Cut 8 strips 2½˝ × WOF (for binding).

Cut 1 strip 1½˝ × WOF.

Black

Cut 1 strip 6½˝ × WOF.

Medium Orange

Cut 1 strip 2½˝ × 16˝.

Cut 1 strip 3˝ × WOF.

Dark Orange

Cut 1 strip 2½˝ × WOF.

Cut 2 strips 2˝ × WOF.

Cut 1 strip 1½˝ × WOF.

Purple

Cut 1 strip 4½˝ × WOF.

Cut 1 strip 2½˝ × WOF.

Cut 1 strip 2˝ × WOF.

Cut 1 strip 1½˝ × WOF.

Dark Blue

Cut 1 strip 3˝ × WOF.

Cut 1 strip 2½˝ × WOF.

Cut 1 strip 1½˝ × WOF.

White

Cut 1 strip 1½˝ × WOF.

CONSTRUCTION

Before beginning any project, read the General Instructions (page 7). This project uses construction techniques for Strip Sets (page 13), Half-Square Triangles (HSTs) (page 11), Combination Triangle units (page 12), and Flying Geese (FG) units (page 13).

Panel Images

Trim all panel images to 6½″ × 6½″. If you are using a larger panel, you may wish to select different traditional patchwork blocks to surround the panel images. Please see Before You Begin (page 7) for suggestions.

Place Mat 1

FINISHED BLOCK: 12″ × 12″

Peony Nine-Patch block variation.

CUTTING

Cut 6 green squares 3½″ × 3½″.

Cut 2 blue squares 3½″ × 3½″. (Cut from 6½″ strip.)

Cut 4 blue rectangles 2½″ × 4½″.

Cut 4 blue squares 2½″ × 2½″.

Cut 1 black rectangle 6½″ × 12½″.

Cut 2 black strips 1½″ × 8½″.

Cut 2 black strips 1½″ × 6½″.

From the yellow strip 3½″ × WOF, cut 2 medium stars, 3 small stars, and 1 crescent moon appliqué shape, using the Small Star, Medium Star, and Crescent Moon templates (page 125).

ASSEMBLY

Press all seam allowances open unless otherwise noted.

1. Sew a black strip 1½″ × 6½″ to the left and right sides of the panel image. Press the seam allowance toward the panel image.

2. Sew a black strip 1½″ × 8½″ to the top and bottom of the panel image. Press the seam allowance toward the panel image.

3. Pair a blue square 3½″ × 3½″ and a green square 3½″ × 3½″ to make 2 HSTs. Make 4 for the block. Press, but **do not trim**.

4. Pair each of the HSTs from Step 1 with a green square 3½″ × 3½″ and follow Step 2 of a Combination Triangle unit (page 12) to make 8 units. Press and trim to 2½″ × 2½″.

5. Arrange 2 units from Step 4 and a blue rectangle 2½″ × 4½″ as shown. Sew together and press the seam allowances toward the rectangle. Make 4. Sew 2 of these units to the left and right sides of the panel. *fig. A*

6. Sew a blue square 2½˝ × 2½˝ to the left and right end of the remaining Step 5 units. Press the seam allowance toward the square. Sew these rows to the top and bottom of the panel, being sure to rotate the bottom row 180°. Press.

7. Appliqué 5 stars and a crescent moon to the black rectangle 6½˝ × 12½˝, using the appliqué method of your choice.

8. Sew the black rectangle to the right side of the Peony Nine-Patch block variation and press the seam allowance toward the black rectangle.

NOTE This block is a variation of a traditional Peony Nine-Patch block. I chose to create space for the panel image by eliminating the center of the block, using the framework around that portion of the block to highlight the panel image.

Peony Nine-Patch

Place Mat 2

FINISHED BLOCK: 12˝ × 12˝

Puss in the Corner block variation.

CUTTING

Cut 1 yellow strip 1½˝ × 16˝.

Cut 8 green rectangles 2˝ × 3½˝.

Cut 2 green squares 2˝ × 2˝.

Cut 2 green squares 1½˝ × 1½˝.

Cut 1 medium orange strip 2½˝ × 16˝.

Cut 2 dark orange rectangles 2½˝ × 4½˝.

Cut 4 dark orange rectangles 2˝ × 6½˝.

Cut 4 dark orange rectangles 2˝ × 3½˝.

Cut 4 dark orange squares 2˝ × 2˝.

Cut 4 dark orange rectangles 1½˝ × 3½˝.

Cut 4 dark orange rectangles 1½˝ × 2½˝.

Cut 1 purple pair (left and right) of Candy Corn B Background triangles from 4½˝ × WOF.

Cut 10 purple squares 2˝ × 2˝.

Cut 2 purple rectangles 1½˝ × 4½˝.

Cut 2 purple squares 1½˝ × 1½˝.

Cut 1 white strip 1½˝ × 16˝.

Use Candy Corn B and Candy Corn B Background templates (page 125).

ASSEMBLY

Press all seam allowances open unless otherwise noted.

1. Sew a dark orange rectangle 2˝ × 6½˝ to the left and right sides of the panel and press toward the panel.

2. Sew a purple square 2˝ × 2˝ to each end of 2 dark orange rectangles 2˝ × 6½˝. Press and add to the top and bottom of the panel. Press the seam allowances toward the panel.

3. Sew a green rectangle 2˝ × 3½˝ to each end of a dark orange rectangle 2˝ × 3½˝ and press. Make 4. Sew 1 unit to the left and right sides of the framed panel and press.

4. Sew a purple square 2˝ × 2˝ to each end of 2 units created in Step 3. Press and add to the top and bottom of the framed panel and press.

5. Construct a strip set from 1 white strip 1½˝ × 16˝, 1 medium orange strip 2½˝ × 16˝, and 1 yellow strip 1½˝ × 16˝. Press the seam allowances toward the orange strip.

6. Using the Candy Corn B template (page 125) or a Tri-Recs tool, cut 3 triangles 4½˝ with the white fabric at the top to make 3 Candy Corns. Set aside 2 Candy Corn triangles for Place Mat 4. *fig. B*

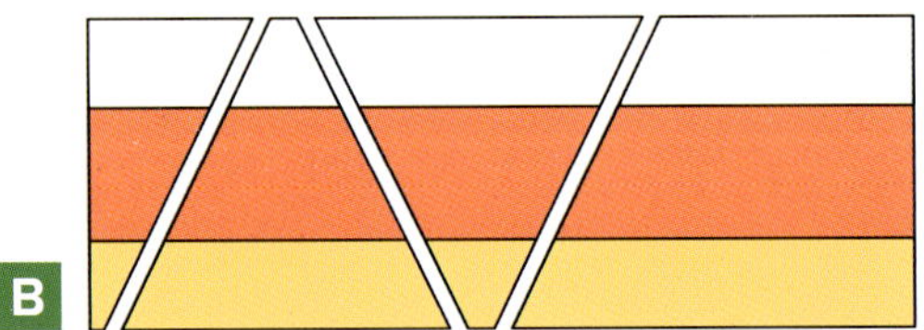

7. Stitch a left and right purple background triangle to each side of the Candy Corn triangle. *fig. C*

8. Sew a purple rectangle 1½˝ × 4½˝ to each side of the Candy Corn. Press the seam allowance toward the rectangles.

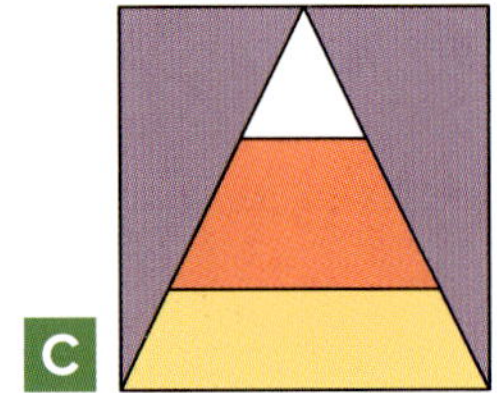

9. Pair a dark orange square 2˝ × 2˝ and a purple square 2˝ × 2˝ to make 2 HSTs. Make a total of 4 HSTs. Press and trim to 1½˝ × 1½˝. Repeat with 2 dark orange squares 2˝ × 2˝ and 2 green squares 2˝ × 2˝ to make 4 HSTs.

10. Construct a Four-Patch by using 2 dark orange/purple HSTs and 2 purple squares 1½˝ × 1½˝. Repeat with 2 dark orange/green HSTs and 2 green squares 1½˝ × 1½˝. *fig. D*

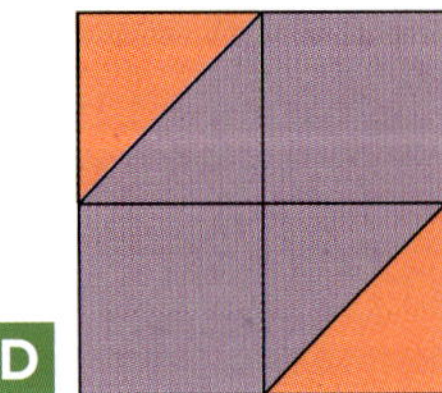

11. Add a dark orange rectangle 1½˝ × 2½˝ to the top and bottom of each Four-Patch.

12. Sew a dark orange/purple HST from Step 9 to the end of each dark orange rectangle 1½˝ × 3½˝. Be sure that the HSTs are oriented correctly. Make 2 more by using the dark orange/green HSTs and the dark orange rectangles. *fig. E*

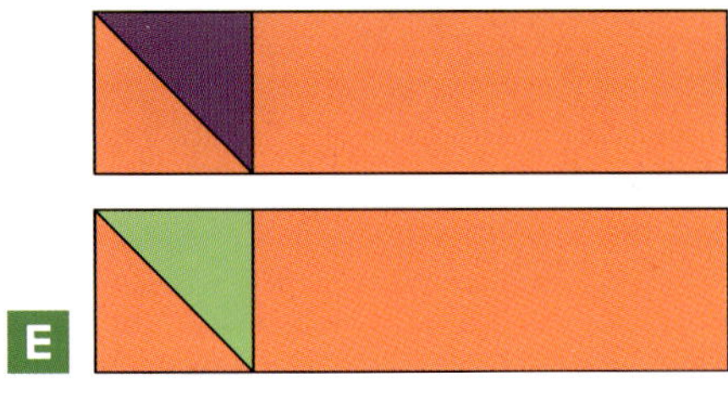

13. Sew these units to each side of the Four-Patch block created in Step 11 to create the Ribbon Candy unit. *fig. F*

14. Sew a dark orange rectangle 2½˝ × 4½˝ to a side of each Ribbon Candy unit.

15. Sew the Ribbon Candy blocks to the top and bottom of the Step 8 Candy Corn block and press. *fig. G*

16. Sew this unit to the right side of the Puss in the Corner variation block and press.

NOTE This block is a variation of a traditional Puss in the Corner block. I chose to create space for the panel image by eliminating the center of the block and the first row of framework around it, using the outer and second framework row to highlight the panel image.

Place Mat 3

FINISHED BLOCK: 12″ × 12″

Weathervane block variation.

CUTTING

Cut 4 yellow squares 3″ × 3″.

Cut 12 yellow squares 2½″ × 2½″.

Cut 1 blue rectangle 6½″ × 12½″.

Cut 4 dark blue squares 3″ × 3″.

Cut 4 purple rectangles 2½″ × 4½″.

Cut 2 purple strips 1½″ × 8½″.

Cut 2 purple strips 1½″ × 6½″.

From the yellow strip 3½″ × WOF, cut 4 small yellow stars, 1 medium star, and 1 crescent moon appliqué shape, using the Small Star, Medium Star, and Crescent Moon templates (page 125).

ASSEMBLY

Press all seam allowances open unless otherwise noted.

1. Sew a purple strip 1½″ × 6½″ to the left and right sides of the panel. Press the seam allowance toward the panel.

2. Sew a purple strip 1½″ × 8½″ to the top and bottom of the panel. Press the seam allowance toward the panel.

3. Pair a purple rectangle 2½″ × 4½″ with 2 yellow squares 2½″ × 2½″ to make an FG unit. Press the seam allowances toward the yellow squares. Make 4.

4. Pair a blue square 3″ × 3″ with a yellow square 3″ × 3″ to make 2 HSTs. Repeat to make 8 HSTs. Press and trim to 2½″ × 2½″.

5. Sew a Step 4 HST to each end of the Step 3 FG units, being sure to orient the HSTs correctly, per the diagram. Make 4. Press the seam allowance toward the FG unit. *fig. H*

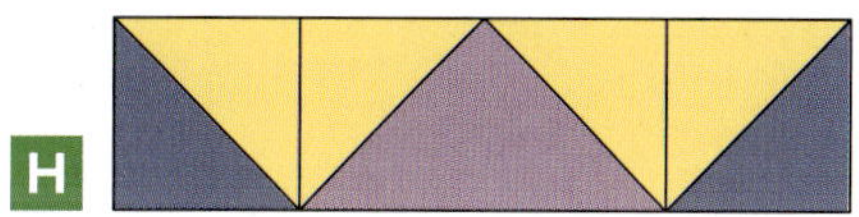

6. Sew a yellow square 2½″ × 2½″ to both ends of 2 of the units sewn in Step 5.

7. Sew the 2 shorter units created in Step 5 to the left and right sides of the panel. Press the seam allowance toward the panel.

8. Sew the Step 6 units to the top and bottom of the panel. Press the seam allowance toward the panel.

9. Appliqué the stars and moon to the blue rectangle 6½″ × 12½″, using the appliqué method of your choice.

10. Sew the blue rectangle to the right side of the Weathervane block variation and press.

Weathervane

Place Mat 4

FINISHED BLOCK: 12″ × 12″

Sister's Choice block variation.

CUTTING

Cut 2 yellow strips 1½″ × 8½″.

Cut 2 yellow strips 1½″ × 6½″.

Cut 6 green squares 3″ × 3″.

Cut 2 green squares 2″ × 2″.

Cut 2 green squares 1½″ × 1½″.

Cut 6 dark blue rectangles 2½″ × 4½″.

Cut 2 dark blue squares 2″ × 2″.

Cut 2 dark blue rectangles 1½″ × 4½″.

Cut 2 dark blue rectangles 1½″ × 3½″.

Cut 2 dark blue rectangles 1½″ × 2½″.

Cut 6 medium orange squares 3″ × 3″.

Cut 8 medium orange squares 2½″ × 2½″.

From the dark blue 4½″ WOF strip, cut 2 pairs (left and right) of background triangles with the Candy Corn B Background template (page 125).

ASSEMBLY

Press all seam allowances open unless otherwise noted.

1. Sew a yellow strip 1½″ × 6½″ to the left and right sides of the panel. Press the seam allowances toward the panel.

2. Sew a yellow strip 1½″ × 8½″ to the top and bottom of the panel. Press the seam allowances toward the panel.

3. Pair a dark blue rectangle 2½″ × 4½″ and 2 medium orange squares 2½″ × 2½″ to sew an FG unit. Press the seam allowances toward the orange squares. Make 4.

4. Pair a green square 3″ × 3″ with a medium orange square 3″ × 3″ to make 2 HSTs. Make a total of 12 HSTs. Press and trim to 2½″ × 2½″.

5. Sew a Step 4 HST to each end of the Step 3 FG units, being sure that HSTs are oriented correctly. Press. Make 4. *fig. I*

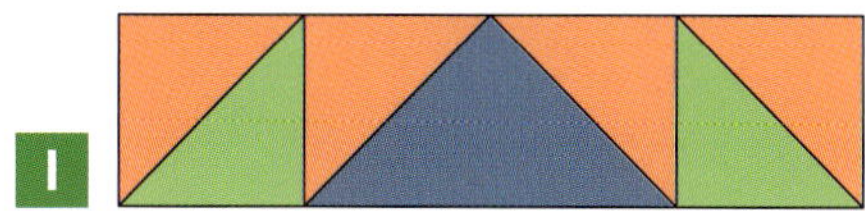

6. Sew a second HST to the left and right ends of 2 of the Step 5 units. Press. *fig. J*

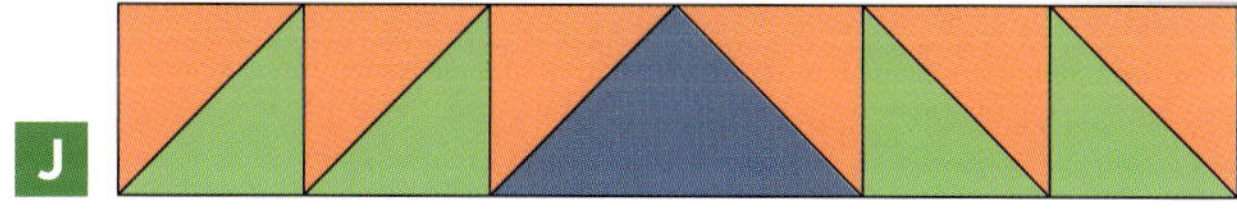

7. Sew a unit created in Step 5 to the left and right sides of the panel. Press.

8. Sew a unit created in Step 6 to the top and bottom of the panel. Press.

9. Pair a dark blue square 2˝ × 2˝ and a green square 2˝ × 2˝ to make 2 HSTs. Press and trim to 1½˝ × 1½˝. Make 4 HSTs.

10. Construct a Four-Patch by using 2 dark blue/green HSTs and 2 green squares 1½˝ × 1½˝. *fig. K*

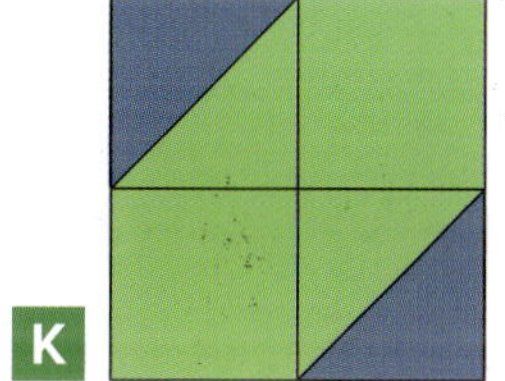

11. Add a dark blue rectangle 1½˝ × 2½˝ to the top and bottom of each Four-Patch.

12. Sew a Step 9 dark blue/green HST to the end of 2 dark blue rectangles 1½˝ × 3½˝. Be sure that HSTs are oriented correctly. *fig. L*

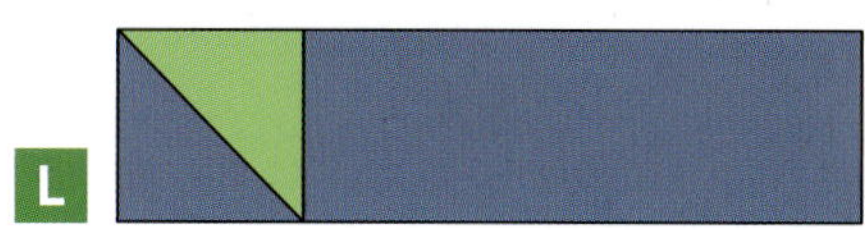

13. Sew these units to each side of the Four-Patch block created in Step 11.

14. Sew a blue strip 1½˝ × 4½˝ to the left and right sides of the Step 13 Ribbon Candy block.

15. Sew blue background triangles to the left and right sides of the remaining 2 Candy Corns created in Place Mat 2 (page 78).

16. Sew a blue rectangle 2½˝ × 4½˝ to the right side of a Candy Corn and a blue rectangle 2½˝ × 4½˝ to the left side of the other Candy Corn. Press the seam allowances toward the rectangles.

17. Sew the Candy Corn with the blue rectangle on the right to the top of the Ribbon Candy block and the Candy Corn with the rectangle on the left to the bottom of the Ribbon Candy block. Press.

18. Sew this unit to the right side of the Sister's Choice block variation and press.

NOTE This block is a variation of a traditional Sister's Choice block. I chose to create space for the panel image by eliminating the squares and rectangles from the center of the block.

Sister's Choice, Option 1

FINISHING

1. Layer each place mat, quilt, and bind.

2. Enjoy!

Make It Your Own!

Sewing and Sowing My Garden by
Susan Wiley

Susan chose the *Love Grows Here* panel and coordinates from Benartex
for her place mats, collectively called *Sewing and Sowing My Garden*.

Susan enhanced her place mats by using elements from several different
patterns she had on hand, all of which focused on the themes found in
the panel images. She created a cheery, bright set of place mats for her
spring and summer table.

Festive Pot Holder

FINISHED POT HOLDER: 8½″ × 8½″

Consider making a few pot holders to complement your table runner and place mats or as a gift for your favorite aspiring chef!

DESIGN SUGGESTIONS

Still got extra panel images? Square them up, add a multicolored border, layer with insulated batting, and you've got a quick and fun gift or useful kitchen accessory. You can also place panel images inside traditional quilt blocks to make great pot holders. Use your imagination and add a little fun to the kitchen!

Materials

Yardages are based on 41″-wide fabrics.

Panel: 1 image adjusted to 7″ × 7″

Yellow: 1 strip 1½″ × 9″

Green: 1 strip 1½″ × 8″

Purple: 1 strip 1½″ × 8″

Orange: 1 strip 1½″ × 7″

Coordinating fabric for loop: 1 strip 2½″ × 8″

Blue: 1 square 9″ × 9″ for backing

Insulated batting: (such as Insul-Bright) 9″ × 9″

CONSTRUCTION

Before beginning any project, read the General Instructions (page 7).

1. Square your panel image by following the instructions in Squaring Up Panel Images (page 7).

2. Sew the orange strip 1½″ × 7″ to the top of the panel image. Press the seam allowance toward the strip. *fig. A*

3. Sew the purple strip 1½″ × 8″ to the right side of the panel image. Press the seam allowance toward the panel image. *fig. B*

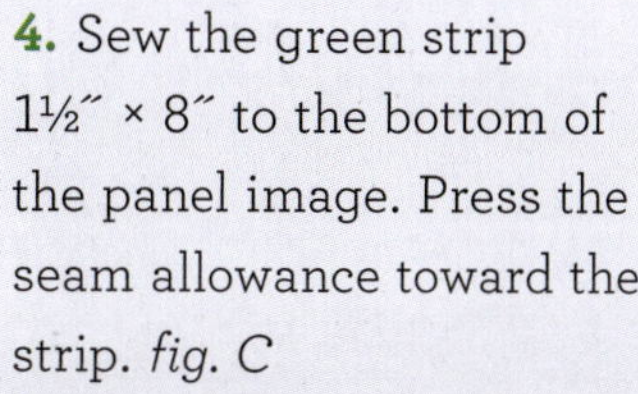

4. Sew the green strip 1½″ × 8″ to the bottom of the panel image. Press the seam allowance toward the strip. *fig. C*

5. Sew the yellow strip 1½″ × 9″ to the left side of the panel image. Press the seam allowance toward the strip.

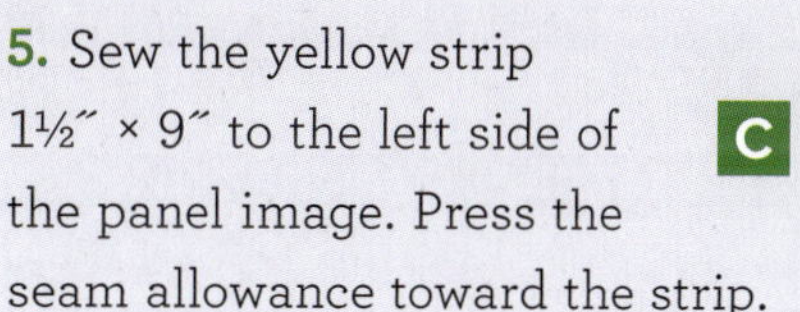

6. Press the coordinating fabric strip 2½″ × 8″ in half, wrong sides together.

7. Open the strip and press each long edge to the center pressed line.

8. Fold the 2 long pressed edges together and topstitch along both edges ⅛″ from the fold.

9. Trim to 5″ long or desired length to use as a hanging loop. *fig. D*

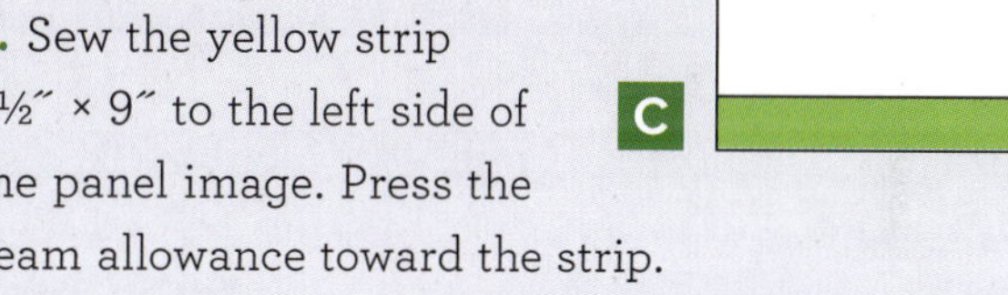

10. Fold the hanging loop in half and pin to the upper-left corner of the pot holder, about ½″ from the left edge, matching raw edges. The fold will be toward the body of the pot holder.

11. Layer the pot holder with the insulated batting on the bottom, the backing right side up, and the top right side down. Pin all the way around. *fig. E*

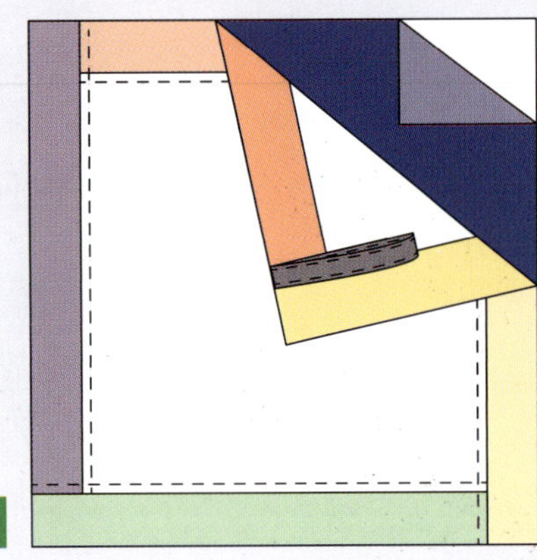

12. Using a ¼˝ seam allowance, begin stitching 4˝ from one corner and continue to ⅜˝ before the next side. Turn to a 45°, Make 1 stitch, turn the corner and continue to sew the next side of the pot holder. Repeat this process at each corner.

13. After stitching the last corner, stop sewing 2½˝ to 3˝ from the beginning so there is an opening to turn your pot holder right side out.

14. Trim away the corners. *fig. F*

15. Turn the pot holder right side out and use a point turner to gently push out the corners.

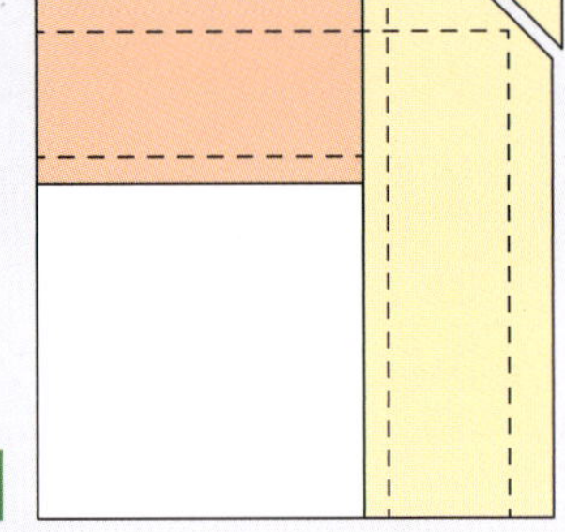

16. Press and whipstitch the opening closed OR topstitch all the way around the pot holder ⅛˝ from the outside edge.

17. Stitch in the ditch between the panel images and the frame strips or quilt as desired.

18. Enjoy!

PROJECTS FOR COMPANION IMAGE PANELS

Companion image panels, those with a variety of image sizes, present a unique challenge, and the panels selected for these projects demonstrate that a little more flexibility is needed when substituting a different panel image than the one shown in the original pattern. Don't let that stop you, though! It can be done, as you'll see from how the contributors worked with the patterns to highlight the panels they chose.

Winter Serenity

FINISHED QUILT: 63″ × 63″

Design Suggestions

I used the *Woodland Winter* panel by Moda Fabrics. The larger central image is square, and the smaller images lent themselves well to being featured in a traditional block. I eliminated the Square in a Square motif in the Union block, inserted the panel images in that space, and then surrounded them with a two-color Flying Geese (snowflake) border. Lots of negative space in the background added to the feeling of a new blanket of snow.

For a completely different look with fewer companion images, take a look at the *Gnome Sweet Gnome* quilt by Tonya Hubbard (page 97), featuring bright colors and playful garden gnomes.

Soft winter snow elicits a feeling of peacefulness, and coupled with the sweet wildlife in this panel, my goal was to create a surround for the central panel that hinted at snowflakes.

Materials

Yardages are based on 41˝-wide fabric

Panel: Multi-image panel with multiple-size images. I used the *Woodland Winter* panel by Moda Fabrics, with its central panel image and 6 companion images.

Cream for background: 2⅝ yards

Black: ½ yard

Dark brown: ⅜ yard

Tan: ½ yard

Red: ¼ yard

Dark green: ⅜ yard

Medium green: ⅛ yard

Blue: ⅞ yard

Binding: ⅝ yard

Backing: 4⅛ yards

Batting: 71˝ × 71˝

Cutting

All rectangles and squares for the individual units and blocks will be subcut from the following strips.

Cream

Cut 7 strips 5˝ × WOF (width of fabric).

Cut 5 strips 3½˝ × WOF.

Cut 2 strips 3˝ × WOF.

Cut 4 strips 2½˝ × WOF.

Cut 8 strips 2˝ × WOF.

Black

Cut 1 strip 3½˝ × WOF.

Cut 1 strip 2½˝ × WOF.

Cut 3 strips 2˝ × WOF.

Dark Brown

Cut 1 strip 2½˝ × WOF.

Cut 3 strips 2˝ × WOF.

Tan

Cut 1 strip 5˝ × WOF.

Cut 1 strip 2½˝ × WOF.

Cut 3 strips 2˝ × WOF.

Red

Cut 1 strip 2½˝ × WOF.

Cut 1 strip 2˝ × WOF.

Dark Green

Cut 1 strip 3½˝ × WOF.

Cut 1 strip 2½˝ × WOF.

Cut 2 strips 2˝ × WOF.

Medium Green

Cut 1 strip 2½˝ × WOF.

Blue

Cut 1 strip 5˝ × WOF.

Cut 1 strip 3½˝ × WOF.

Cut 2 strips 3˝ × WOF.

Cut 3 strips 2˝ × WOF.

Cut 4 strips 1½˝ × WOF.

Binding

Cut 7 strips 2½˝ × WOF.

CONSTRUCTION

Before beginning any project, read the General Instructions (page 7). This project uses Half-Square Triangles (HSTs) (page 11), Snowball Corners (page 13), and Flying Geese (FG) units (page 13).

Every small companion panel image in this quilt is framed in a different-color variation of a Union Square block and then surrounded by a complementary-color snowflake frame. The Union Square block has a great space where panel images can be highlighted.

Panel Images

Adjust the large center panel to 22½˝ × 22½˝. Be sure that the panel is squared up before trimming! See Panel Preparation (page 7) for how to adjust the panel images to this size.

Adjust the 6 smaller companion panel images to 6½˝ × 6½˝.

CUTTING

Cut 2 blue strips 1½˝ × 24½˝.
Cut 2 blue strips 1½˝ × 22½˝.

ASSEMBLY

Press all seam allowances open unless otherwise noted.

1. Sew blue strips 1½˝ × 22½˝ to the left and right sides of the central large panel.

2. Sew blue strips 1½˝ × 24½˝ to the top and bottom of the central large panel.

Union Square Setting

FINISHED BLOCK: 9˝ × 9˝

For small panel images.

Make 2 each of block 1, block 2, and block 3.

CUTTING

Cut 48 cream squares 2½˝ × 2½˝.

Cut 24 cream squares 2˝ × 2˝.

From each color (black, dark brown, tan, red, dark green, medium green):

Cut 8 squares 2½˝ × 2½˝.

BLOCK 1 ASSEMBLY

Make 2: 1 dark brown (left) and 1 tan (right). These blocks are placed at the center of each side.

1. Pair a dark brown square 2½˝ × 2½˝ with a cream square 2½˝ × 2½˝ to make 2 HSTs. Make 16 dark brown/cream HSTs. Press and trim to 2˝ × 2˝.

2. Arrange 4 dark brown/cream HSTs as shown and sew together. Make 4. *fig. A*

3. Sew a unit made in Step 2 to the left and right sides of a small

panel image. Press the seam allowances toward the panel image.

4. Add 2 cream squares 2˝ × 2˝ to the ends of the remaining Step 2 units. *fig. B*

5. Sew the top and bottom rows to the small panel image, rotating as shown. Press the seam allowances toward the panel image. *fig. C*

6. Repeat Steps 1–5 with tan and cream squares for the second panel image.

BLOCK 2 ASSEMBLY

Make 2: 1 dark green (right) and 1 red (left). These blocks are placed in the upper left and right of the central panel image.

For the upper-right block:

1. Pair a dark green square 2½˝ × 2½˝ with a cream square 2½˝ × 2½˝ to make 2 HSTs. Make 16 green HSTs. Press and trim to 2˝ × 2˝.

2. Sew 4 dark green/cream HSTs in a row, orienting the HSTs as illustrated. Make 4. *fig. D*

A 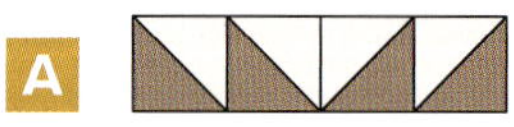

B 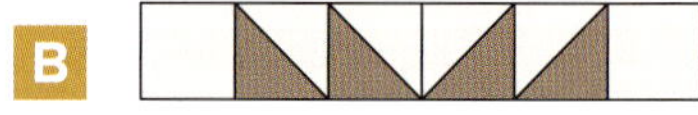

C 

D 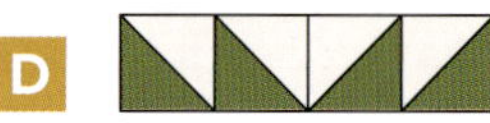

3. Sew 2 of the units made in Step 2 to the left and right sides of a small panel image. Press the seam allowance toward the panel image.

4. Assemble only the top row of the block, adding 2 cream squares 2˝ × 2˝ to each end of a Step 2 unit. *fig. E*

5. Sew the top row to the small panel image. Press the seam allowance toward the panel image. *fig. F*

TIP
DO NOT add a bottom row to this block.

6. Sew a cream square 2˝ × 2˝ to the right end of the last row created in Step 2. Set aside for Section B: Upper Right, Step 3 (page 92). *fig. G*

7. Repeat Steps 1–6 for the red and cream squares for the upper-left block. Then, for Step 6, sew the cream square to the **left** end of the last row created in Step 2. Set aside for Section B: Upper Left, Step 3 (page 91).

BLOCK 3 ASSEMBLY

Make 2: 1 medium green (left) and 1 black (right). These blocks are placed in the lower left and right of the central panel image.

For the lower left block:

1. Pair a medium green square 2½˝ × 2½˝ with a cream square 2½˝ × 2½˝ to make 2 HSTs. Make 16 medium green HSTs. Press and trim to 2˝ × 2˝.

2. Sew 4 medium green/cream HSTs 2˝ × 2˝ in a row, orienting the HSTs as illustrated. Make 4. *fig. H*

3. Sew 2 units made in Step 2 to the left and right sides of a small panel image. Press the seam allowances toward the panel image.

4. Sew 2 cream squares 2˝ × 2˝ to a unit from Step 2, as shown. *fig. I*

5. Sew the row to the bottom of the small panel image. Press the seam allowance toward the panel image. *fig. J*

TIP
DO NOT add a top border to this block.

6. Sew a cream square 2˝ × 2˝ to the left end of the last row created in Step 2. Set aside for Section B: Lower Left, Step 3 (page 93). *fig. K*

7. Repeat Steps 1–6 with black and cream squares for the lower-right panel image. In Step 6, sew the cream square to the **right** end of the last black row. Set aside for Section B: Lower Right, Step 3 (page 93).

Snowflake Frame Block 1

FINISHED BLOCK: 15˝ × 15˝

Make 2: 1 blue (left) and 1 black (right) for the center-row blocks.

CUTTING

Cut 8 cream squares 3½˝ × 3½˝.

Cut 24 cream rectangles 2˝ × 3½˝, subcut from 3½˝ × WOF.

Cut 48 cream squares 2˝ × 2˝.

Cut 12 black rectangles 2˝ × 3½˝, subcut from 3½˝ × WOF.

Cut 28 black squares 2˝ × 2˝ black.

Cut 12 blue rectangles 2˝ × 3½˝, subcut from 3½˝ × WOF.

Cut 28 blue squares 2˝ × 2˝.

ASSEMBLY

Press all seam allowances open unless otherwise noted.

1. Pair a cream rectangle 2˝ × 3½˝ and 2 blue squares 2˝ × 2˝ to sew an FG unit (page 13). Make 12.

2. Pair a blue rectangle 2˝ × 3½˝ and 2 cream squares 2˝ × 2˝ to sew an FG unit. Make 12.

E 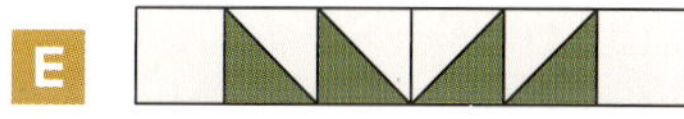

F 

G 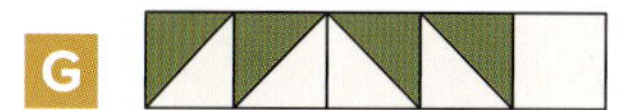

H 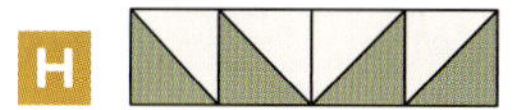

I 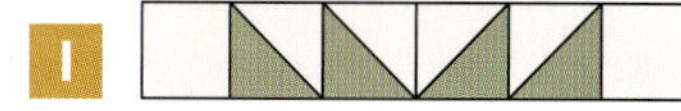

J 

K 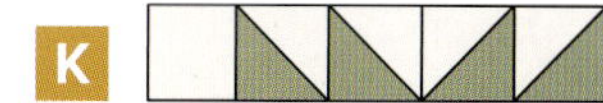

3. Using a cream square 3½˝ × 3½˝ and a blue square 2˝ × 2˝, sew a Snowball Corner (page 13) to a square. Make 4. *fig. L*

4. Pair an FG from Steps 1–2 as shown and sew together to make a Double FG block. Make 12. *fig. M*

5. Assemble the left- and right-side rows of the Snowflake Frame as illustrated, using 3 Double FG blocks. Sew 3 Double FG blocks together as shown. Make 4. *fig. N*

6. Assemble the top and bottom rows of the Snowflake Frame as illustrated, using a Step 5 unit and 2 Snowball Corners. Make 2. *fig. O*

7. Sew the Step 5 side rows to the left and right sides of the left small panel image with the dark brown Union Square Frame. *fig. P*

8. Sew the Step 6 rows to the top and bottom of the block. *fig. Q*

9. Repeat Steps 1–8 with the black and cream squares for the right small panel image with the tan Union Square Frame.

Snowflake Frame Block 2

SECTION A
FINISHED SECTION A: 19½˝ × 15˝

Make 2: 1 dark green (left) and 1 dark brown (right) for the upper-row blocks.

Cutting

Cut 2 cream rectangles 5˝ × 15½˝.

Cut 2 cream squares 5˝ × 5˝.

Cut 3 cream squares 3½˝ × 3½˝.

Cut 9 cream rectangles 2˝ × 3½˝, subcut from 3½˝ × WOF.

Cut 4 cream squares 2½˝ × 2½˝.

Cut 18 cream squares 2˝ × 2˝.

Cut 9 dark green rectangles 2˝ × 3½˝, subcut from 3½˝ × WOF.

Cut 4 dark green squares 2½˝ × 2½˝.

Cut 21 dark green squares 2˝ × 2˝.

Assembly

Press all seam allowances open unless otherwise noted.

1. Pair a cream rectangle 2˝ × 3½˝ and 2 dark green squares 2˝ × 2˝ to sew an FG unit. Make 9.

2. Pair a dark green rectangle 2˝ × 3½˝ and 2 cream squares 2˝ × 2˝ to sew an FG unit. Make 9.

3. Pair a Step 1 and a Step 2 FG and sew together to make a Double FG block. Make 9.

4. Pair a dark green square 2½˝ × 2½˝ with a cream square 2½˝ × 2½˝ to make 2 HSTs. Make 8. Press and trim to 2˝ × 2˝.

5. Pair 2 HSTs as illustrated and sew together. Label as pair A. Make 2. *fig. R*

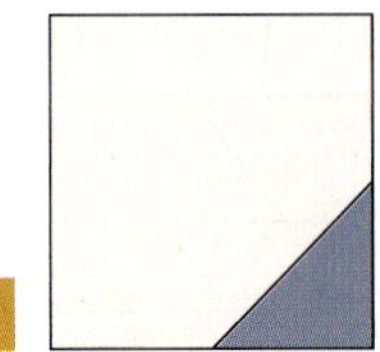

L

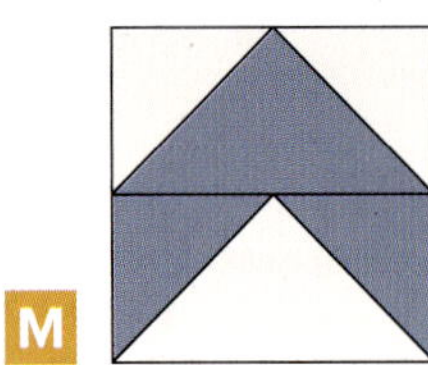

M

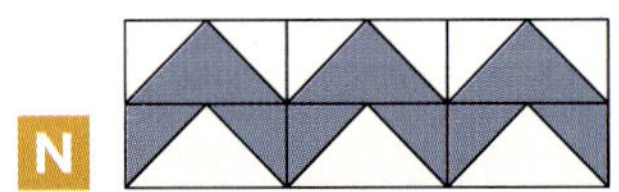

N

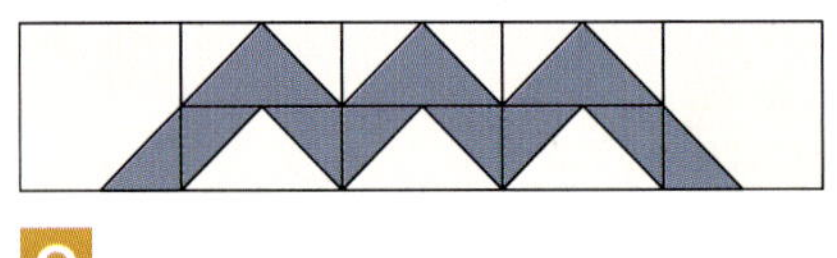

O

P

Q

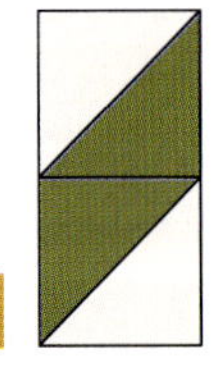

R

6. Arrange 2 Double FG blocks and a pair A unit as shown. Sew together and press. Sew this row to the right side of the red Union Square Frame block 2. *fig. S*

7. Pair 2 HSTs as illustrated. Label as pair B. Make 2. *fig. T*

8. Sew a pair B unit to the left end of a row of 2 Double FG blocks, as shown. Press. Sew this unit to the left side of the Step 6 block. *fig. U*

9. Using a cream square 3½˝ × 3½˝ and a dark green square 2˝ × 2˝, sew a single Snowball Corner to the square. Make 3. Press. *fig. V*

10. Sew a Snowball Corner block to each end of a row of 3 double FG blocks being careful to orient the Snowball Corners and the squares correctly as illustrated for the top row of the frame. *fig. W*

11. Sew the top row to the top of the Step 8 block. *fig. X*

12. Sew a cream rectangle 5˝ × 15½˝ to the top of the Step 11 block. Press the seam allowance toward the rectangle.

13. Sew a cream rectangle 5˝ × 15½˝ to the left side of the Step 12 block. Press the seam allowance toward the rectangle. *fig. Y*

14. Repeat Steps 1–13 with the dark brown and cream squares for the upper-right tan Union Square Frame block 2. This includes cutting, substituting the dark brown for the dark green. For Step 13, sew the second cream rectangle to the **right** side of the block.

SECTION B: UPPER LEFT
FINISHED SECTION B: 15˝ × 4½˝

1. Sew a pair B unit to the right end of a row of 2 Double FG blocks as illustrated for the bottom row of the frame. Press. *fig. A*

2. Sew a Snowball Corner block to the left end of this row. *fig. B*

3. Sew a pair A unit to the end of the last row of the Union Square block that you set aside previously in Block 2 Assembly, Step 6 (above), as illustrated. *fig. C*

4. Sew the Step 2 unit to the bottom of the Step 3 unit. *fig. D*

5. Sew a cream square 5˝ × 5˝ to the left end of the Step 4 unit. Sew this row to the **top** of the blue Snowflake Frame block 1. *fig. E*

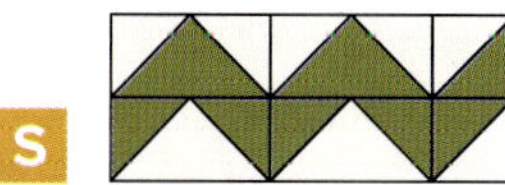
S

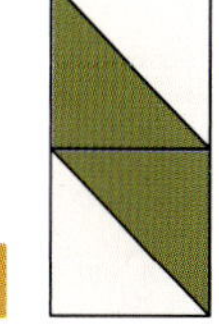
T

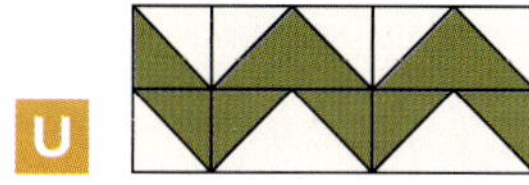
U

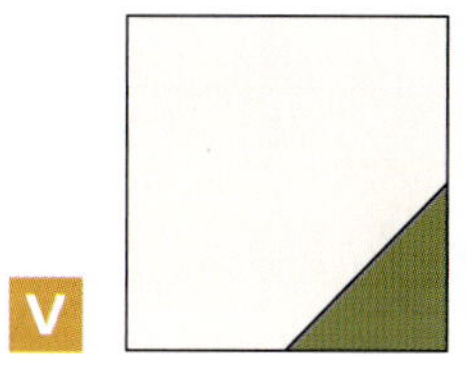
V

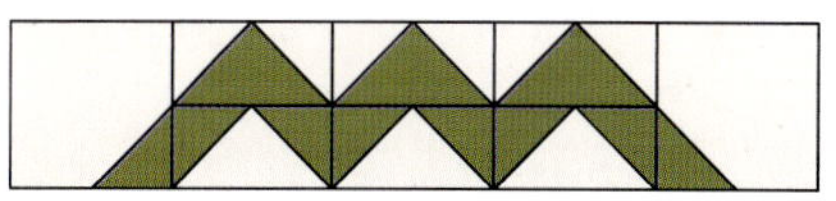
W

X

Y

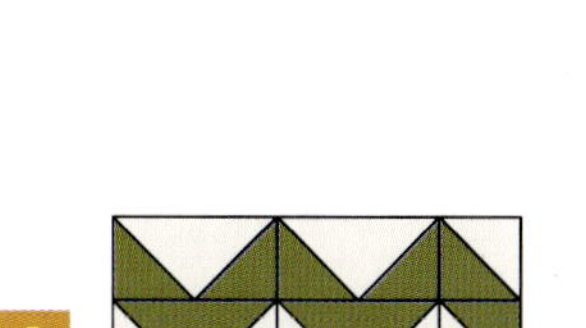
A

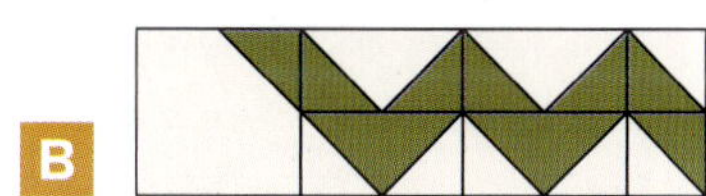
B

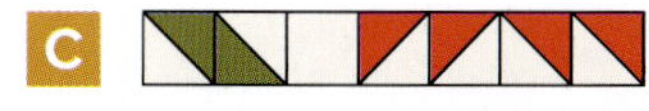
C

D

E

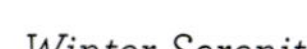

FINISHED SECTION B: 4½˝ × 15˝

1. Sew a pair A unit to the left end of a row of 2 Double FG blocks as illustrated for the bottom row of the frame. Press. *fig. A*

2. Sew a Snowball Corner block to the right end of this row. *fig. B*

3. Sew a pair B unit to the end of the last row of the Union Square block that you set aside previously in Block 2 Assembly, Step 5 (page 89), being sure to orient as illustrated. *fig. C*

4. Sew the Step 2 unit to the bottom of the Step 3 unit. *fig. D*

5. Sew a cream square 5˝ × 5˝ to the right end of the Step 4 unit. *fig. E*

6. Sew this unit to the **top** of the black Snowflake Frame block 1.

Snowflake Frame Block 3

SECTION A

FINISHED SECTION A: 10½˝ × 15˝

Make 2: 1 tan (left) and 1 red (right) for the lower-row blocks.

Cutting

Cut 2 cream rectangles 5˝ × 15½˝. Cut 4 cream squares 2½˝ × 2½˝.

Cut 1 cream square 5˝ × 5˝. Cut 18 cream squares 2˝ × 2˝.

Cut 3 cream squares 3½˝ × 3½˝. Cut 4 tan squares 2½˝ × 2½˝.

Cut 9 cream rectangles 2˝ × 3½˝, subcut from 3½˝ × WOF. Cut 9 tan rectangles 2˝ × 3½˝.

Cut 21 tan squares 2˝ × 2˝.

Assembly

1. Pair a cream rectangle 2˝ × 3½˝ and 2 tan squares 2˝ × 2˝ to sew an FG unit. Make 9. Press.

2. Pair a tan rectangle 2˝ × 3½˝ and 2 cream squares 2˝ × 2˝ to sew an FG unit. Make 9. Press.

3. Pair a Step 1 and a Step 2 FG and sew together to make a Double FG block. Press. Make 9.

4. Pair a tan square 2½˝ × 2½˝ with a cream square 2½˝ × 2½˝ to make 2 HSTs. Make 8. Press and trim to 2˝ × 2˝.

5. Pair 2 HSTs as illustrated. Label as pair A. Make 2. *fig. F*

6. Sew a pair A unit to the right end of a row of 2 Double FG blocks as illustrated. Sew this unit to the left side of the medium green Union Square Frame block 3. *fig. G*

7. Pair 2 HSTs as shown and sew together. Press. Label as pair B. Make 2. *fig. H*

8. Sew a pair B unit to the left end of a row of 2 Double FG blocks as illustrated and sew to the right side of the Step 6 block. *fig. I*

9. Using a cream square 3½˝ × 3½˝ and a tan square 2˝ × 2˝, sew a single Snowball Corner to the square. Make 3. Press. *fig. J*

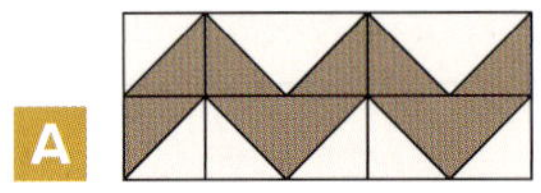

A

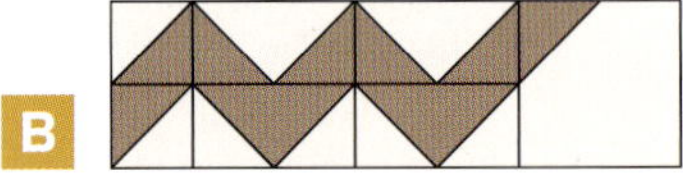

B

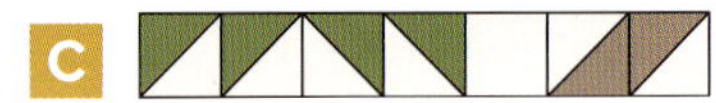

C

D

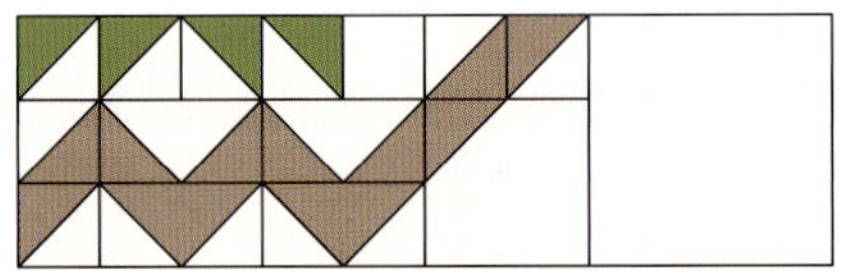

E

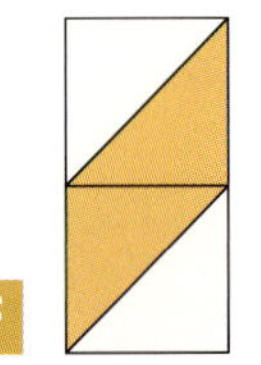

F

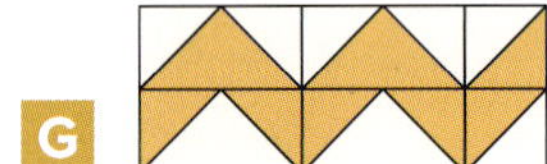

G

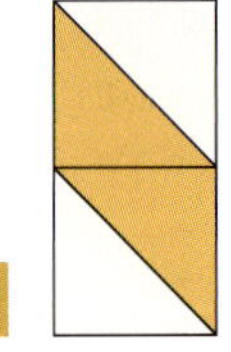

H

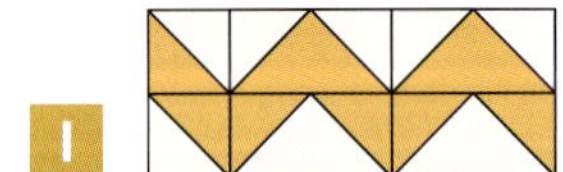

I

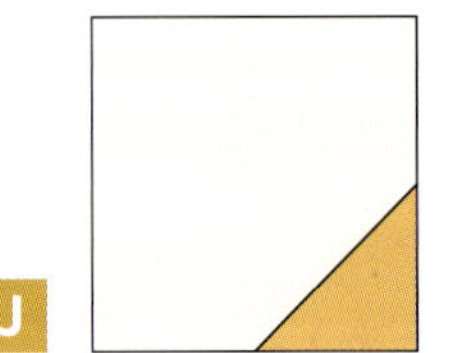

J

10. Sew a Snowball Corner block to each end of a row of 3 Double FG blocks as illustrated for the bottom row of the frame. *fig. K*

11. Sew the Step 10 row to the bottom of the Step 8 block. *fig. L*

12. Sew a cream rectangle 5″ × 15½″ to the bottom of the Step 11 block. Press the seam allowance toward the rectangle.

13. Sew a cream rectangle 5″ × 15½″ to the left side of the Step 12 block. Press the seam allowance toward the rectangle. *fig. M*

14. Repeat Steps 1–13 with the red and cream squares for the black Union Square Frame Block 3. Note that for this lower-right block, in Step 13, the rectangle will be sewn to the **right** side of the block.

SECTION B: LOWER LEFT ASSEMBLY
FINISHED SECTION B: 4½″ × 15″

1. Sew a pair A unit to the right end of a row of 2 Double FG blocks as illustrated for the top row of the frame. Press. *fig. N*

2. Sew a Snowball Corner block to the left end of this unit. *fig. O*

3. Sew a pair B unit to the left end of the last row of the Union Square block that you set aside previously in Block 3 Assembly, Step 6 (page 89). *fig. P*

4. Sew the Step 2 unit to the top row of the Step 3 unit. *fig. Q*

5. Sew a cream square 5″ × 5″ to the left end of the Step 4 unit. Sew this row to the **bottom** of Snowflake Frame block 1. *fig. R*

SECTION B: LOWER RIGHT ASSEMBLY
FINISHED SECTION B: 4½″ × 15″

1. Sew a pair B unit to the left end of a row of 2 Double FG blocks as illustrated for the top row of the frame. Press. *fig. S*

2. Sew a Snowball Corner block to the right end of this row. *fig. T*

3. Sew a pair A unit to the right end of the last row of the Union Square block that you set aside previously in Block 3 Assembly, Step 7 (page 89). *fig. U*

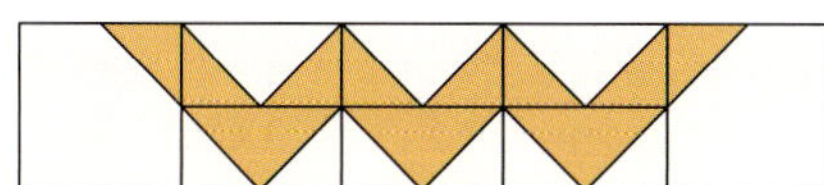

K

L

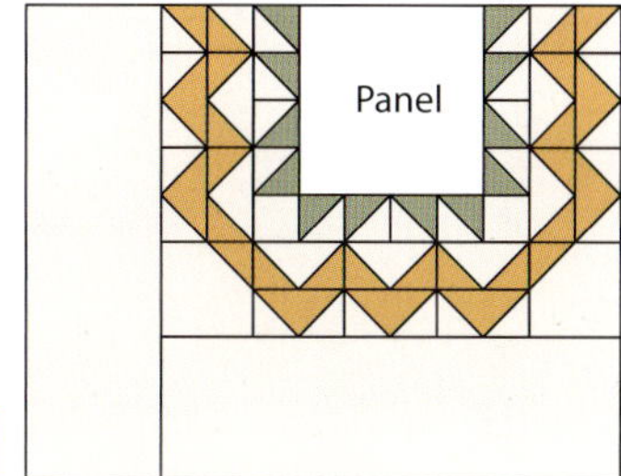

M

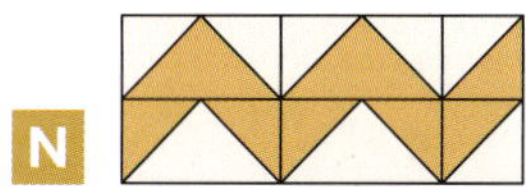

N

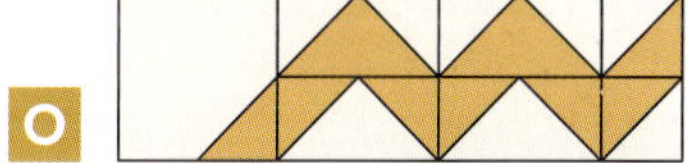

O

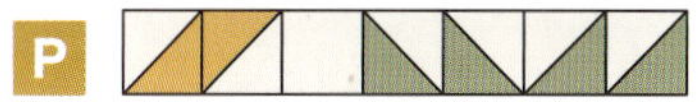

P

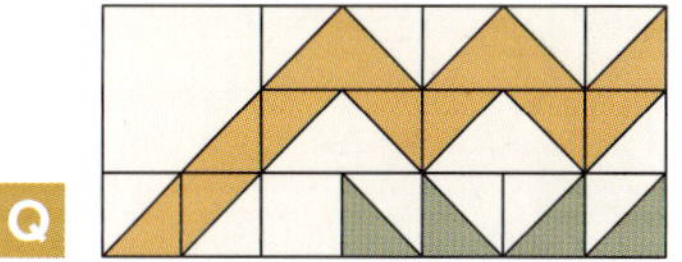

Q

R

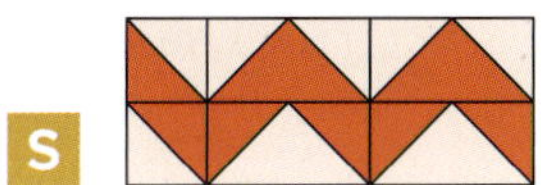

S

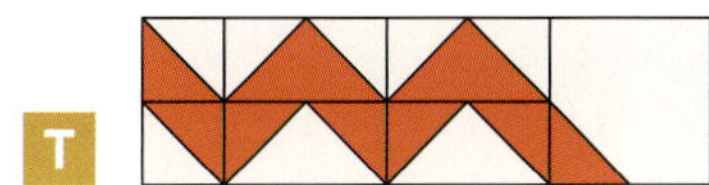

T

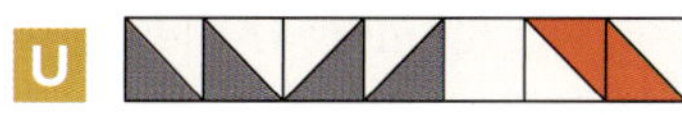

U

4. Sew the Step 2 unit to the top of the Step 3 unit. *fig. V*

5. Sew a cream square 5˝ × 5˝ to the right end of the top row. Sew this row to the **bottom** of Snowflake Frame block 1. *fig. W*

Union Square Block

FINISHED BLOCK: 15˝ × 15˝

Make 2.

CUTTING

Cut 16 cream squares 3˝ × 3˝.

Cut 8 cream squares 2½˝ × 2½˝.

Cut 4 dark brown rectangles 2˝ × 15½˝.

Cut 4 dark brown rectangles 2˝ × 12½˝.

Cut 4 tan squares 5˝ × 5˝.

Cut 4 blue squares 5˝ × 5˝.

Cut 16 blue squares 3˝ × 3˝.

ASSEMBLY

1. Pair a blue square 5˝ × 5˝ and a tan square 5˝ × 5˝ to make 2 HSTs. Make 8. Press and trim to 4½˝ × 4½˝.

2. Arrange 4 blue/tan HSTs as shown. Sew the HSTs together to form the center of the block. Make 2. *fig. A*

3. Pair a blue square 3˝ × 3˝ and a cream square 3˝ × 3˝ to make 2 HSTs. Make 32 HSTs for the frame of the block. Press and trim to 2½˝ × 2½˝.

4. Arrange 4 blue/cream HSTs as shown. Sew together and press. Make 8. *fig. B*

5. Sew 4 of the Step 4 sets to the left and right sides of the block centers.

6. Sew the top and bottom rows of each block by using 2 cream squares 2½˝ × 2½˝ and the remaining Step 4 units as shown. Press. Make 4. *fig. C*

7. Sew the Step 6 top and bottom rows of HSTs to the top and bottom of the Step 5 block. *fig. D*

8. Sew a dark brown strip 2˝ × 12½˝ to each side of the Union Square block. Press. Make 2.

8. Sew a dark brown strip 2˝ × 15½˝ to the top and bottom of each Union Square block. Press. Make 2. *fig. E*

V

W

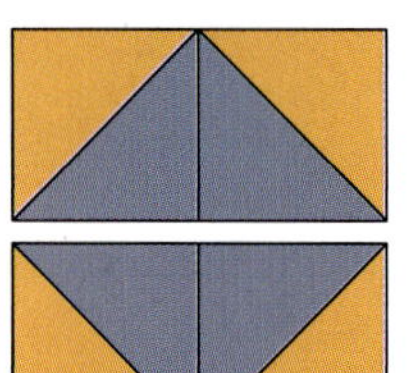

A

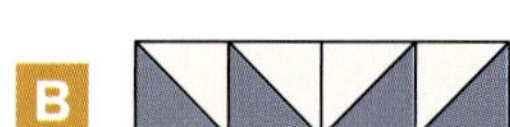

B

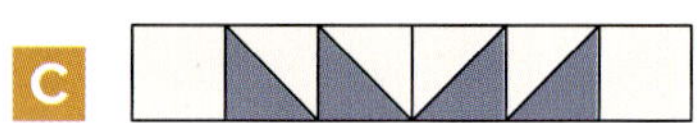

C

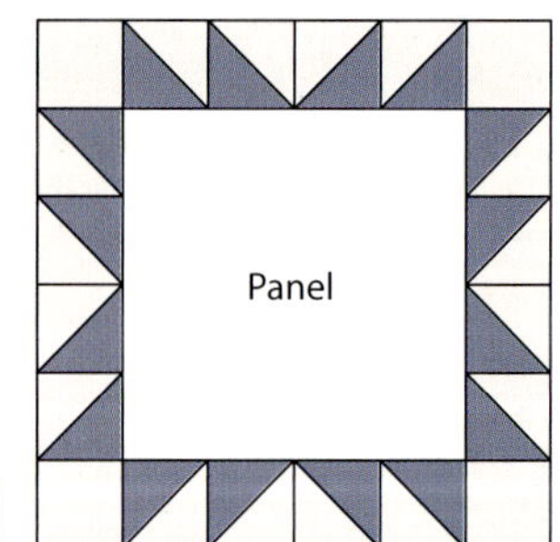

D

E

Quilt Top Assembly

Press all seam allowances open unless otherwise noted.

1. Sew the top row of the quilt by using the upper-left Snowflake block 2, a framed Union Square block, and the upper-right Snowflake block 2. *fig. F*

2. Sew the center row of the quilt by using Snowflake block 1 on the left and right sides of the center panel. Be sure your color placement is correct to ensure that the Snowflake Frame is all the same color. *fig. G*

3. Sew the bottom row of the quilt by using the lower-left Snowflake block 3, a framed Union Square block, and the lower-right Snowflake block 3. Press. *fig. H*

4. Sew the rows together and press.

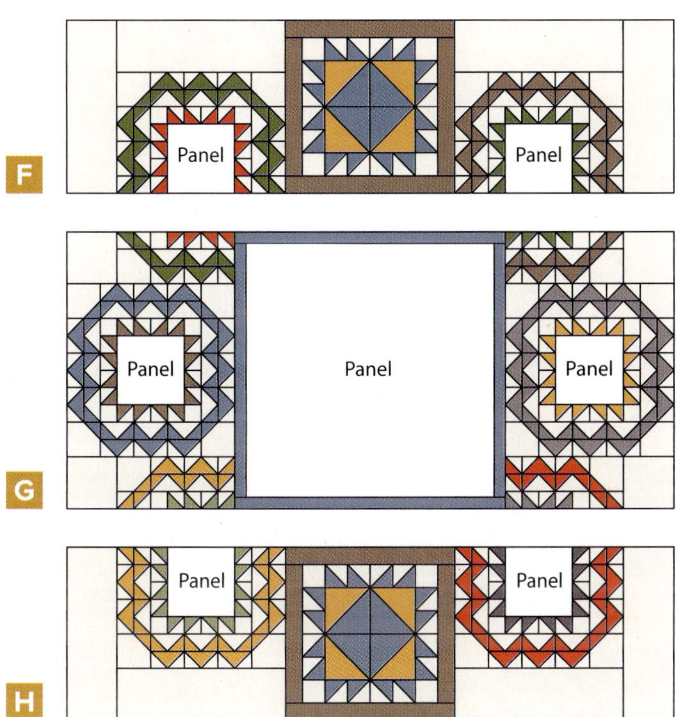

OUTER BORDERS

Cutting

From each color (black, dark brown, tan, red, dark green, blue):

Cut 4 rectangles 2˝ × 3½˝, subcut from 2˝ × WOF.

Cut 8 squares 2˝ × 2˝.

Cut 4 cream rectangles 5˝ × 36½˝.

Cut 4 cream squares 5˝ × 5˝.

Cut 24 cream rectangles 2˝ × 3½˝, subcut from 3½˝ × WOF.

Cut 4 cream rectangles 2˝ × 12½˝.

Cut 4 cream rectangles 2˝ × 6½˝.

Cut 48 cream squares 2˝ × 2˝.

Assembly

Press all seam allowances open unless otherwise noted.

1. Pair a dark green rectangle 2″ × 3½″ and 2 cream squares 2″ × 2″ to make an FG unit. Make 4 each of dark green, dark brown, red, blue, black, and tan. Press.

2. Pair a cream rectangle 2″ × 3½″ and 2 dark green squares 2″ × 2″ to make an FG unit. Make 4 each of dark green, dark brown, red, blue, black, and tan. Press.

3. Pair an FG from Step 1 and Step 2 to sew a Double FG block as illustrated. Make 4 each of dark green, dark brown, red, blue, black, and tan.

4. Arrange 2 pairs of tan Double FG blocks together, rotating the second block 180°, and a cream rectangle 2″ × 6½″ as shown. Sew together and press. Make 2. *fig. A*

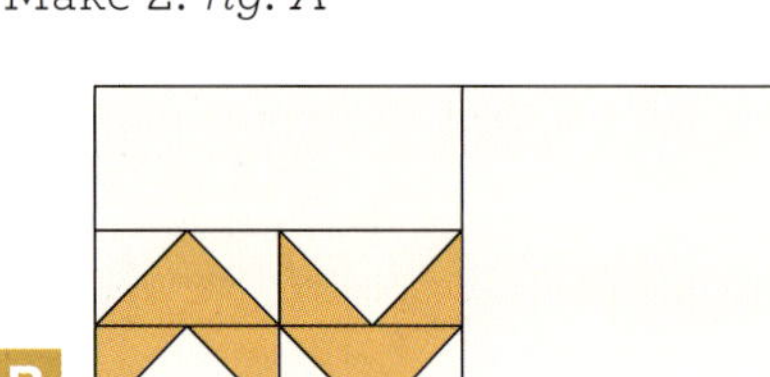

5. Sew a cream square 5″ × 5″ to a Step 4 unit and set aside for the top border. Make 2. *fig. B*

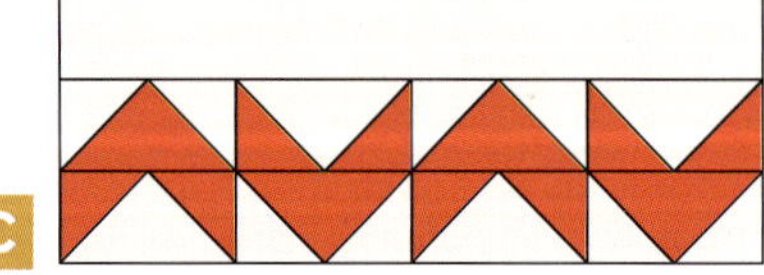

6. Repeat Steps 4–5 with the dark brown sets of FG for the bottom border.

7. Arrange 4 red Double FG blocks, alternating every other block 180°, and a cream rectangle 2″ × 12½″ as shown. Sew together and press. *fig. C*

8. Repeat Step 7 with the dark green, black, and blue sets of Double FG blocks.

9. Sew a cream square 5″ × 5″ to the left end of the Step 7 red and Step 8 dark green FG units. *fig. D*

10. Sew a dark brown Step 4 unit to a cream rectangle 5″ × 36½″. Add the Step 7 unit to the other end of the cream rectangle. Press. *fig. E*

E   Left border: Dark brown and black

11. Repeat Step 10 with a tan and blue set. *fig. F*

F   Right border: Tan and blue

12. Sew the Steps 10–11 borders to the left and right sides of the quilt top. Refer to the diagram for color placement. Press.

13. Sew a dark brown unit of 2 FG from Step 5 to a cream 5″ × 36½″ strip. Add the dark green FG unit from Step 8 to the other end of this cream strip for the bottom border. Press. Repeat with the tan and red units for the top border. Be sure to orient the elements correctly. *figs. G–H*

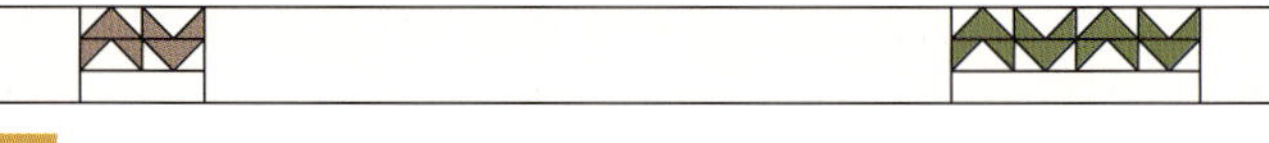

G   Bottom border: Dark brown and dark green

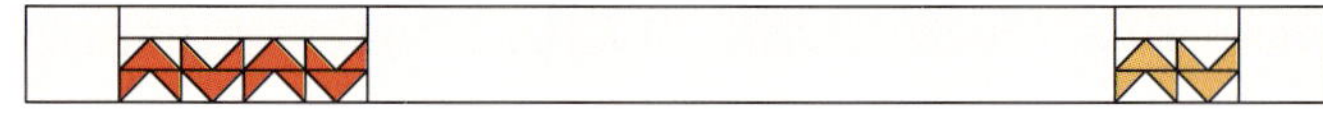

H   Top border: Red and tan

Finishing

1. Layer, quilt, and bind as desired.

2. Enjoy!

Make It Your Own!

Gnome Sweet Gnome by Tonya Hubbard

Tonya chose the *Gnome Grown* panel and an assortment of coordinates by Wilmington Prints. Because there were only 4 coordinating images that were a large size, she altered the instructions by increasing the number of HSTs in the surround for the panel images. She chose to incorporate the original Union Square block in 4 corners around the quilt and the images in the center of each row and column.

Coffee, Tea, or Cocoa?

FINISHED QUILT: 33″ × 48″

Design Suggestions

This quilt is based on a panel featuring a smaller central image with small coordinating images. It could easily be adapted to accommodate a larger central panel with coordinating images, as Heikei Kovacich did in *Liam's Quilt*, adapted from this project (page 103).

There's nothing like your favorite hot drink on a crisp fall morning or a snowy winter day. Using a variety of simple geometric shapes and a single panel with its coordinating smaller images, I had fun creating a wall hanging to grace my coffee bar!

Materials

Yardages are based on 41˝-wide fabrics.

Panel: Multiple-image panel featuring a smaller main image (approximately 18˝ × 32˝) with 4 or more companion images adjustable to 5˝ × 5˝. I used the *Perfect Brew* panel from Benartex.

Beige: ⅜ yard

Black: 1 yard

Red: ⅜ yard

Tan: ½ yard for binding

Backing: 1⅝ yards

Batting: 41˝ × 56˝

Cutting

All rectangles and squares for the individual blocks will be subcut from the following strips.

Beige

Cut 3 strips 2½˝ × WOF (width of fabric).

Cut 1 strip 2˝ × WOF.

Black

Cut 3 strips 2½˝ × WOF.

Cut 12 strips 2˝ × WOF.

Red

Cut 4 strips 2˝ × WOF.

Tan

Cut 5 strips 2½˝ × WOF (binding).

CONSTRUCTION

Before beginning any project, read the General Instructions (page 7). This project uses construction techniques for Strip Sets (page 13), Half-Square Triangles (HSTs) (page 11), and Flying Geese (FG) units (page 13).

Panel Images

Adjust your panel images so that the large center panel is 15½˝ × 30½˝ and the 4 smaller panel segments are 5˝ × 5˝; refer to Panel Preparation (page 7) to adjust your panels to size.

For my chosen panel, I needed to trim the main and smaller segments to fit in the designated spaces.

Block 1

FINISHED BLOCK 1: 7½˝ × 7½˝

Make 4.

CUTTING

Cut 8 black squares 2½˝ × 2½˝.

Cut 8 beige squares 2½˝ × 2½˝.

ASSEMBLY

Press all seam allowances open unless otherwise noted.

1. Construct a strip set as shown by using 2 black strips 2˝ × WOF and a red strip 2˝ × WOF. Press and label this strip set A.

2. From strip set A, subcut 16 units 2˝ × 5˝. Set aside the remainder of the strip set for Block 3. *fig. A*

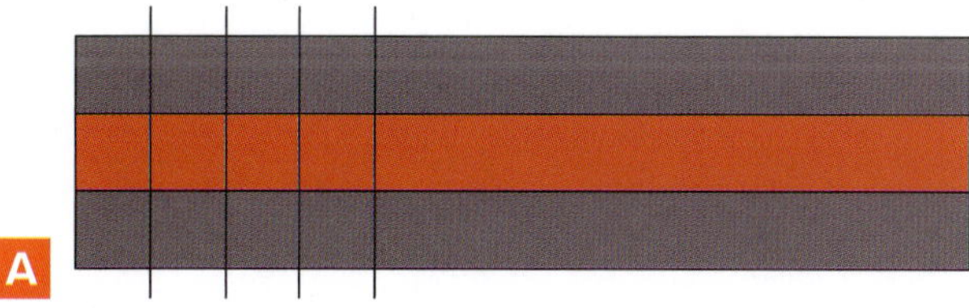

3. Pair a black square 2½˝ × 2½˝ and a beige square 2½˝ × 2½˝, right sides together, and sew together to create 2 HSTs. Make 16. Press and trim to 2˝ × 2˝.

4. Sew a strip set A unit to the left and right sides of each small panel image.

5. Sew a Step 3 HST to each end of 2 strip set A units, carefully aligning the direction of the HSTs as shown. Make 8. One of these rows will be rotated 180° for each block. *fig. B*

6. Sew a row created in Step 5 to the top and bottom of the block, checking that HSTs are positioned correctly.

Block 2

FINISHED BLOCK: 7½˝ × 3˝

Make 8.

CUTTING

Cut 8 beige squares 2½˝ × 2½˝.

Cut 16 black rectangles 2˝ × 3½˝.

Cut 8 black squares 2½˝ × 2½˝.

Cut 8 black squares 2˝ × 2˝.

ASSEMBLY

Press all seam allowances open unless otherwise noted.

1. Construct a second strip set A with 2 black strips 2˝ × WOF and a red strip 2˝ × WOF. Subcut 6 units 2˝ × 5˝. Set aside the remainder of the strip set for Block 3.

2. Pair a black square 2½˝ × 2½˝ and a beige square 2½˝ × 2½˝, right sides together, and sew to create 2 HSTs. Make 16. Press and trim to 2˝ × 2˝.

3. Sew an HST on each side of a 2˝ × 2˝ black square. Make 8. *fig. C*

4. Sew a strip set A unit to each HST unit created in Step 2, orienting the HST correctly as shown. Make 8. *fig. D*

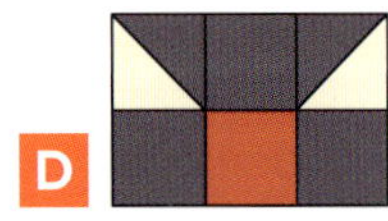

5. Sew a black rectangle 2˝ × 3½˝ to each end of the unit assembled in Step 4. Make 8.

Block 3

FINISHED BLOCK: 7½˝ × 7½˝

Make 4.

CUTTING

Cut 16 beige squares 2½˝ × 2½˝.

Cut 16 black squares 2½˝ × 2½˝.

Cut 24 black squares 2˝ × 2˝.

Cut 8 red squares 2˝ × 2˝.

ASSEMBLY

Press all seam allowances open unless otherwise noted.

1. From the remaining sections of strip set A from Blocks 1 and 2, subcut 4 units 2˝ × 5˝.

2. Pair a black square 2½˝ × 2½˝ and a beige square 2½˝ × 2½˝, right sides together, and sew to create 2 HSTs. Make 32 HSTs. Press and trim to 2˝ × 2˝.

3. Construct a strip set as shown by using 2 red strips 2˝ × WOF and a black strip 2˝ × WOF. Press and label this as strip set B. Subcut 8 units 2˝ × 5˝. Set aside the remainder of the strip set for Block 5. *fig. E*

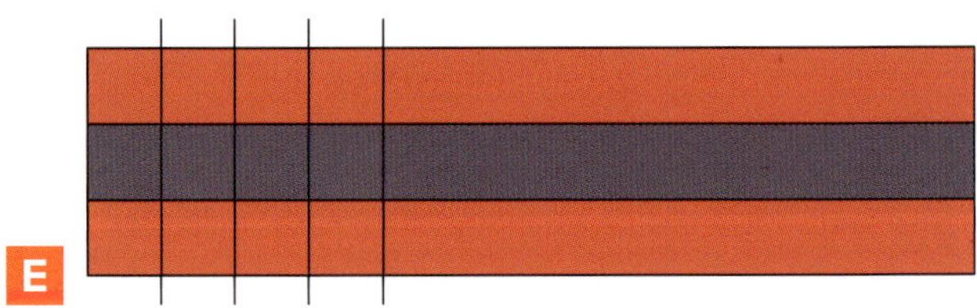

4. Using 3 black squares 2˝ × 2˝ and 2 HSTs, construct the row as shown. Make 8. Half of these rows will be rotated 180°. *fig. F*

5. Using 2 strip set B units and a strip set A unit, sew a Nine-Patch block. *fig. G*

6. Using a red square 2˝ × 2˝ and 2 HSTs, construct the row as shown. Make 8. Half of these rows will be rotated 180°. *fig. H*

7. Sew a unit constructed in Step 6 to each side of the Nine-Patch, orienting the HSTs as shown. *fig. I*

8. Sew a row constructed in Step 4 to the top and bottom of the block, rotating the bottom row.

Block 4

FINISHED BLOCK: 7½˝ × 9˝

Make 2.

CUTTING

Cut 4 beige squares 2½˝ × 2½˝.

Cut 4 beige rectangles 2˝ × 3½˝.

Cut 4 black squares 2½˝ × 2½˝.

Cut 20 black squares 2˝ × 2˝.

Cut 8 black rectangles 2˝ × 3½˝.

Cut 6 red rectangles 2˝ × 3½˝.

Cut 8 red squares 2˝ × 2˝.

ASSEMBLY

Press all seam allowances open unless otherwise noted.

1. Pair a beige rectangle 2˝ × 3½˝ with 2 black squares 2˝ × 2˝ to construct an FG unit. Make 4.

2. Pair a black square 2½˝ × 2½˝ and a beige square 2½˝ × 2½˝, right sides together, and sew to create 2 HSTs. Make 8. Press and trim to 2˝ × 2˝.

3. Using 3 black squares 2˝ × 2˝ and 2 HSTs, construct the row as shown. Make 4. One of these rows will be rotated 180°. *fig. J*

4. Using a red square 2˝ × 2˝ and 2 black rectangles 2˝ × 3½˝, construct the row as shown. Make 4. Set aside the remaining 4 red squares 2˝ × 2˝ for the borders. *fig. K*

5. Using 3 red rectangles 2˝ × 3½˝ and 2 Step 1 FG units, construct the row as shown. Make 2. *fig. L*

6. Sew a row created in Step 3 to the top and bottom of the units created in Step 5, being sure to rotate one row 180°.

7. Sew the rows created in Step 4 to the top and bottom of the blocks as shown.

Block 5

FINISHED BLOCK: 9˝ × 7½˝

Make 2.

CUTTING

Cut 8 beige squares 2½˝ × 2½˝.

Cut 4 beige rectangles 2˝ × 3½˝.

Cut 8 black squares 2½˝ × 2½˝.

Cut 4 black rectangles 2˝ × 3½˝.

Cut 20 black squares 2˝ × 2˝.

Cut 2 red rectangles 2˝ × 3½˝.

ASSEMBLY

Press all seam allowances open unless otherwise noted.

1. Subcut 4 units 2˝ × 5˝ from the remaining strip set B created in Block 3.

2. Pair a beige rectangle 2˝ × 3½˝ with 2 black squares 2˝ × 2˝ to construct an FG unit. Make 4.

3. Using 2 black squares 2˝ × 2˝, 2 HSTs, and a Step 2 FG unit, construct a row as shown. Make 4. *fig. M*

4. Sew an HST to each side of a black square 2˝ × 2˝ as shown, being careful to orient the HSTs correctly. Make 4. *fig. N*

5. Sew each of these units to a strip set B unit from Step 1. *fig. O*

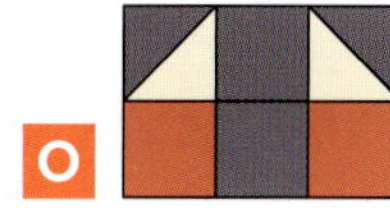

6. Sew 2 black rectangles 2˝ × 3½˝ to both sides of a red rectangle 2˝ × 3½˝. Make 2. *fig. P*

7. Sew the Step 5 units to each side of the Step 6 unit as shown.

8. Sew the Step 3 units to the top and bottom of each Step 7 unit.

Quilt Top Assembly

1. Following the quilt assembly diagram, construct each top and bottom border by using 2 Block 2s and 1 Block 5. Make 2. Add the top and bottom borders to the central panel.

2. Following the quilt assembly diagram, construct each side border by using 2 Block 1s, 2 Block 2s, 2 Block 3s, and 1 Block 4. Make 2. Add these borders to the left and right sides of the central panel.

Add Outer Borders

1. Sew a black strip 2˝ × 45½˝ to each side of the quilt body.

2. Sew a red square 2˝ × 2˝ (cut in Block 4) to each end of the black strip 2˝ × 30½˝.

3. Add these borders to the top and bottom of the quilt. *fig. Q*

Q Quilt assembly

FINISHING

1. Quilt, bind, and add a hanging sleeve, as desired.

2. Enjoy!

<h1 style="text-align:center">Make It Your Own!</h1>

For a fun addition to this project, consider making some mug rugs to coordinate with the wall hanging! Check out the bonus projects on page 104.

Liam's Quilt by Heikei Kovacich features a larger set of panels than the original project called for. To make everything work, Heikei simply changed all the squares and HSTs from 1½˝ to 2˝ and the Flying Geese from 1½˝ × 3˝ to 2˝ × 4˝. She was able to trim the panel images to work with these units as well.

Heikei chose the *Kitty Couple* panel from Loralie Designs and added bright solids from her stash.

Mug Mats

FINISHED MAT: 6″ × 6″

For a fun stocking stuffer or quick gift, use your leftover panel images or fussy cut some companion fabrics to feature in a quick mug mat!

DESIGN SUGGESTIONS

If you have leftover panel images and want a quick project, fussy cut a portion of the panel image to fit into a small space within a traditional block. Here, I've used a 6″ × 6″ Churn Dash block, but a Sawtooth Star 6″ × 6″ and other traditional blocks with adequate center space will work as well.

Materials

Yardages are based on 41˝-wide fabric and will yield 4 mug mats

Panel: 4 panel images adjustable to 2½˝ × 2½˝. I used *The Perfect Brew* by Benartex.

Red: ¼ yard or fat quarter

Tan: ¼ yard or fat quarter

Coordinating print for backing: ¼ yard or fat quarter

Batting: 4 pieces 6½˝ × 6½˝

Cutting

Panel

Trim and square a panel image (or fussy cut from coordinating print) 2½˝ × 2½˝.

Red

Cut 2 squares 3˝ × 3˝.

Cut 1 strip 1½˝ × 11˝.

Tan

Cut 2 squares 3˝ × 3˝.

Cut 1 strip 1½˝ × 11˝.

Coordinating Print

Cut a square coordinating print 6˝ × 6˝.

CONSTRUCTION

Before beginning any project, read the General Instructions (page 7). This project uses construction techniques for Strip Sets (page 13) and Half-Square Triangles (HSTs) (page 11).

1. Sew a red strip 1½˝ × 11˝ and a tan strip 1½˝ × 11˝ to create a strip set. Press the seam allowance toward the red strip.

2. Subcut the strip set to create 4 squares 2½˝ × 2½˝.

3. Pair a red square 3˝ × 3˝ and a tan square 3˝ × 3˝ to make 2 HSTs. Make 4 HSTs for the block. Press and trim to 2½˝ × 2½˝.

4. Lay out the block and sew 3 rows. Press the seam allowances in the top and bottom rows open. Press the middle-row seam allowances toward the panel image. Sew the rows together and press. *fig A*

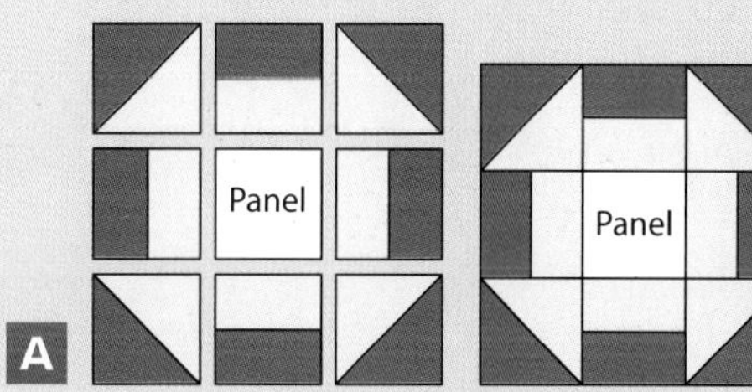

5. Layer a square of batting 6½˝ × 6½˝ with the backing square 6½˝ × 6½˝, right side up. Lay the right side of the block to the right side of the backing fabric. Pin all sides.

6. Begin sewing 2˝ before the corner on one side. Be sure to backstitch.

7. Stop stitching ⅜˝ before the corner, turn the mat 45°, and make a stitch.

8. Turn the mat and continue stitching the next side. Repeat the diagonal stitch at all 4 corners.

9. Upon returning to the first side sewn, stop stitching 2˝ after turning the corner and backstitch, leaving an opening to turn your mat right side out. Clip the points off each corner to reduce bulk. Use a point turner to create crisp points. Press the mat, being sure to turn in the unsewn edges.

10. Hand stitch the opening closed. Quilt, if desired.

Cat Nap

Design Suggestions

This quilt showcases the *Kitty the Cat* panel from Clothworks, featuring a large central image and several coordinating images. I framed each kitty with a modified Rosebud block, but any block with an outer framework could be substituted. See *Chirping Christmas* by Terry Helmer (page 117).

A colorful background of various-size rectangles sets off the multi-image panel in this quilt. Any medium or large panel can be substituted; see Preparing Panel Images (page 7).

Materials

Yardages are based on 41˝-wide fabric.

Panel: Multi-image panel featuring a large central image (approximately 16˝ × 20˝) with 4 or more companion images adjustable to 8˝ × 8˝. I used the *Kitty the Cat* panel from Clothworks.

White for background: 2⅜ yards

Gray: ⅝ yard

Green: ½ yard

Dark blue: ¾ yard

Medium blue: ½ yard

Orange: ⅝ yard

Yellow: ¾ yard

Binding: ⅝ yard

Backing: 4⅝ yards

Batting: 80˝ × 82˝

Cutting for Blocks and Columns

All background rectangles listed in the instructions below will be cut from these strips.

White

Cut 9 strips 4½˝ × WOF (width of fabric).

Cut 4 strips 3½˝ × WOF.

Cut 4 strips 2½˝ × WOF for side borders.

Cut 8 strips 1½˝ × WOF for top and bottom borders.

Gray

Cut 1 strip gray 8½˝ × WOF.

Cut 3 strips gray 4½˝ × WOF.

Green

Cut 2 strips green 4½˝ × WOF.

Cut 1 strip green 3½˝ × WOF.

Dark Blue

Cut 3 strips dark blue 4½˝ × WOF.

Cut 1 strip dark blue 3½˝ × WOF.

Cut 1 strip dark blue 2½˝ × WOF.

Medium Blue

Cut 2 strips medium blue 4½˝ × WOF.

Cut 1 strip medium blue 3½˝ × WOF.

Orange

Cut 3 strips orange 4½˝ × WOF.

Cut 1 strip orange 3½˝ × WOF.

Yellow

Cut 3 strips yellow 4½˝ × WOF.

Cut 1 strip yellow 3½˝ × WOF.

Cut 1 strip yellow 2½˝ × WOF.

Binding

Cut 8 strips 2½˝ × WOF.

CONSTRUCTION

Before beginning any project, read the General Instructions (page 7). This project uses construction techniques for Coping Strips (page 9) and Half-Square Triangles (HSTs) (page 11).

Panel Images

FINISHED CENTER PANEL:
28″ × 18″

FINISHED COMPANION IMAGES:
8″ × 8″

1. Adjust the large center panel to 28½″ × 18½″. If necessary, coping strips can be added to reach this measurement.

2. Adjust the smaller panel images to 8½″ × 8½″.

NOTE See the suggestions at the end of this project for how to construct this quilt with fewer companion images.

Rose Bud

FINISHED BLOCK: 12″ × 12″

Make 6.

Following instructions in *The Skill-Building Quick & Easy Block Tool* by Debbie Rodgers (by C&T Publishing), I manipulated the outer portions of this block

so that the center square would accommodate a square panel image 8½″ × 8½″.

CUTTING

Cut 24 gray rectangles 1½″ × 8½″, subcut from 8½″ × WOF (width of fabric).

Cut 24 gray rectangles 1½″ × 4½″, subcut from 4½″ × WOF.

Cut 24 dark blue rectangles 1½″ × 2½″, subcut from 2½″ × WOF.

Cut 48 yellow rectangles 1½″ × 2½″, subcut from 2½″ × WOF.

ASSEMBLY

Press all seam allowances open unless otherwise noted.

1. Sew a yellow rectangle 1½″ × 2½″ to each end of a gray rectangle 1½″ × 4½″. Make 24. *fig. A*

2. Sew a gray rectangle 1½″ × 8½″ to 12 of the Step 1 units.

3. Sew a Step 2 unit to both sides of a panel image 8½″ × 8½″. Make 6. Press the seam allowance toward the panel.

4. Sew a dark blue rectangle 1½″ × 2½″ to each end of the 12 remaining Step 1 units. *fig. B*

5. Sew a medium blue strip 1½″ × WOF to a dark blue strip 1½″ × WOF to create a strip set. Press the seam allowance toward the dark blue.

6. Subcut 24 units 1½″ × 2½″ from the strip set.

7. Sew 2 Step 6 units to each end of a gray rectangle 1½″ × 8½″, with the dark blue strip touching the gray rectangle. Make 12. *fig. C*

8. Sew a Step 7 unit to a Step 4 unit. Make 12.

9. Sew a Step 8 unit to the top and bottom of each Step 3 panel image. Make 6.

CUTTING COLUMN A

Cut rectangles 4½″ × 7½″: 2 white, 1 gray, 1 dark blue, 1 orange.

Cut rectangles 4½″ × 5½″: 3 white, 1 gray, 1 medium blue.

Cut rectangles 4½″ × 3½″: 1 orange, 1 yellow.

COLUMN A ASSEMBLY

Sew all rectangles together along the short 4½″ edge.

1. Sew a white rectangle 4½″ × 5½″ (piece 1) to an orange rectangle 4½″ × 7½″ (piece 2).

2. Sew a white rectangle 4½″ × 5½″ (piece 3) to a gray rectangle 4½″ × 7½″ (piece 4).

3. Sew a medium blue rectangle 4½″ × 5½″ (piece 5) to a white rectangle 4½″ × 7½″ (piece 6).

4. Sew an orange rectangle 4½″ × 3½″ (piece 7) to a white rectangle 4½″ × 7½″ (piece 8).

5. Sew a gray rectangle 4½″ × 5½″ (piece 9)

to a yellow rectangle
4½″ × 3½″ (piece 10).

6. Sew a white rectangle
4½″ × 5½″ (piece 11)
to a dark blue rectangle
4½″ × 7½″ (piece 12).

7. Sew all the pairs of rectangles
together in order. Press all seam
allowances toward piece 12. Set
this column aside.

CUTTING COLUMN E

Cut rectangles 4½″ × 7½″: 2 white,
1 gray, 1 orange.

Cut rectangles 4½″ × 5½″: 2 white,
1 green, 1 dark blue, 1 yellow.

Cut square 4½″ × 4½″: 1 yellow.

Cut rectangles 4½″ × 3½″: 1 gray,
1 green, 1 medium blue.

COLUMN E ASSEMBLY

Sew all rectangles together
along the short 4½″ edge.

1. Sew a yellow square
4½″ × 4½″ (piece 1)
to a white rectangle
4½″ × 7½″ (piece 2).

2. Sew a dark
blue rectangle
4½″ × 5½″ (piece 3)
to a green rectangle
4½″ × 3½″ (piece 4).

3. Sew a white rectangle
4½″ × 7½″ (piece 5)
to a gray rectangle
4½″ × 3½″ (piece 6).

4. Sew a white rectangle
4½″ × 5½″ (piece 7)
to a green rectangle
4½″ × 5½″ (piece 8).

5. Sew a gray rectangle
4½″ × 7½″ (piece 9)

to a yellow rectangle
4½″ × 5½″ (piece 10).

6. Sew an orange rectangle
4½″ × 7½″ (piece 11) to
a medium blue rectangle
4½″ × 3½″ (piece 12).

7. Sew all the pairs together in
order and add a white rectangle
4½″ × 5½″ (piece 13) to the end.
Press all seam allowances toward
piece 13. Set this column aside.

CUTTING SECTION 1

Cut rectangles 4½″ × 7½″: 3 white,
1 dark blue, 1 orange, 1 yellow.

Cut rectangles 4½″ × 5½″: 1 white,
1 gray, 1 dark blue, 1 medium
blue.

Cut square 4½″ × 4½″: 1 yellow.

Cut rectangles 4½″ × 3½″: 1 white,
1 green.

SECTION 1 ASSEMBLY

There are 3 short columns that
make up this section. Each
column will begin with a new
piece 1. Sew all rectangles
together along the short 4½″ edge.

1. Sew a white rectangle
4½″ × 7½″ (piece 1) to a yellow
rectangle 4½″ × 7½″ rectangle
(piece 2).

2. Sew a white rectangle
4½″ × 7½″ (piece 3) to a green
rectangle 3½″ × 4½″ (piece 4).

3. Sew the pairs together and
press the seam allowances in this
column toward piece 1. Set aside.

4. Sew a dark blue rectangle
4½″ × 5½″ (piece 1) to a gray
rectangle 4½″ × 5½″ (piece 2).

5. Sew a white rectangle
4½″ × 7½″ (piece 3) to a dark blue
rectangle 4½″ × 7½″ (piece 4).

6. Sew the pairs together and
press the seam allowances in this
column toward piece 4. Set aside.

7. Sew a yellow square
4½″ × 4½″ (piece 1) to a
medium blue rectangle
4½″ × 5½″ (piece 2).

8. Sew a white rectangle
4½″ × 3½″ (piece 3) to an orange
rectangle 4½″ × 7½″ (piece 4).

9. Sew the pairs together
and add a white rectangle
4½″ × 5½″ (piece 5) to the end.
Press the seam allowances in this
column toward piece 1.

10. Sew the 3 columns from
Steps 3, 6, and 9 together and
press.

CUTTING SECTION 2

Cut rectangles 4½″ × 8½″: 1 white,
1 dark blue.

Cut rectangles 4½″ × 7½″: 3 white,
1 gray, 1 medium blue, 1 yellow.

Cut rectangles 4½″ × 5½″: 2 white,
1 gray, 1 dark blue.

Cut rectangles 4½″ × 3½″: 1 white,
1 green, 2 orange.

SECTION 2 ASSEMBLY

There are 3 short columns that make up this section. Each column will begin with a new piece 1. Sew all rectangles together along the short 4½˝ edge.

1. Sew a white rectangle 4½˝ × 8½˝ (piece 1) to a dark blue rectangle 4½˝ × 5½˝ (piece 2).

2. Sew a medium blue rectangle 4½˝ × 7½˝ (piece 3) to a white rectangle 4½˝ × 7½˝ (piece 4).

3. Sew the pairs together and add an orange rectangle 3½˝ × 4½˝ (piece 5) to the end. Press the seam allowances in this column toward piece 1. Set aside.

4. Sew a white rectangle 4½˝ × 5½˝ (piece 1) to a yellow rectangle 4½˝ × 7½˝ (piece 2).

5. Sew a white rectangle 4½˝ × 3½˝ (piece 3) to an orange rectangle 4½ × 3½˝ (piece 4).

6. Sew a white rectangle 4½˝ × 7½˝ (piece 5) to a gray rectangle 4½˝ × 5½˝ (piece 6).

7. Sew the pairs together and press the seam allowances in this column toward piece 6. Set aside.

8. Sew a dark blue rectangle 4½˝ × 8½˝ (piece 1) to a white rectangle 4½˝ × 5½˝ (piece 2).

9. Sew a gray rectangle 4½˝ × 7½˝ (piece 3) to a green rectangle 4½˝ × 3½˝ (piece 4).

10. Sew the pairs together and add a white rectangle 4½˝ × 7½˝ (piece 5) to the end. Press the seam allowances toward piece 1.

11. Sew the 3 columns from Steps 3, 7, and 10 together and press.

SECTIONS 1–2 ASSEMBLY

Refer to the quilt assembly diagram (page 115).

1. Sew Section 1 to the top of a Rose Bud Frame panel image.

2. Sew Section 2 to the bottom of this Rose Bud Frame panel image.

3. Press the seam allowances away from the Rose Bud Frame panel image.

CUTTING COLUMN B

Cut rectangles 4½˝ × 7½˝: 2 white, 1 gray.

Cut rectangles 4½˝ × 5½˝: 1 white, 1 green, 1 orange.

Cut square 4½˝ × 4½˝: 1 medium blue.

Cut rectangle 4½˝ × 3½˝: 1 dark blue.

COLUMN B ASSEMBLY

Sew all rectangles together along the short 4½˝ edge.

1. Sew a gray rectangle 4½˝ × 7½˝ (piece 1) to a white rectangle (piece 2) 4½˝ × 7½˝.

2. Sew a dark blue rectangle 4½˝ × 3½˝ (piece 3) to a green rectangle 4½˝ × 5½˝ (piece 4).

3. Sew a white rectangle 4½˝ × 7½˝ (piece 5) to an orange rectangle 4½˝ × 5½˝ (piece 6).

4. Sew a white rectangle 4½˝ × 5½˝ (piece 7) to a medium blue square 4½˝ × 4½˝ (piece 8).

5. Sew the pairs together in order and press the seam allowances toward piece 1. Set aside.

CUTTING SECTION 3

Cut rectangle 4½˝ × 8½˝: 1 white.

Cut rectangles 4½˝ × 5½˝: 1 white, 1 dark blue, 1 medium blue, 1 orange, 1 yellow.

Cut rectangles 4½˝ × 3½˝: 2 white.

SECTION 3 ASSEMBLY

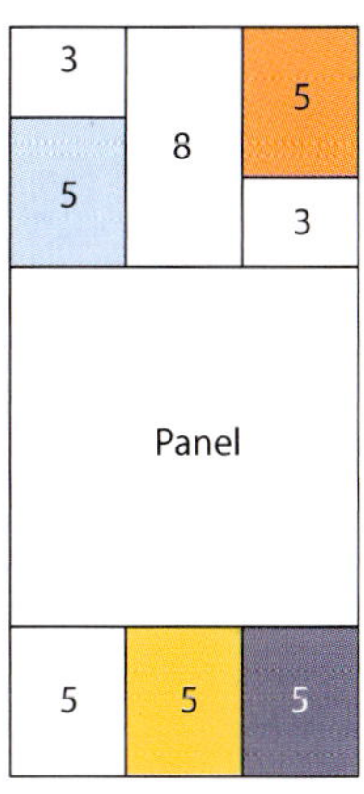

Sew all rectangles together along the short 4½˝ edge unless otherwise noted.

1. Sew a white rectangle 4½˝ × 3½˝ (piece 1) to a medium blue rectangle 4½˝ × 5½˝ (piece 2). Press the seam allowance toward piece 2.

2. Sew the Step 1 unit to a white rectangle 4½˝ × 8½˝ along the left *long edge*. Press.

3. Sew an orange rectangle 4½˝ × 5½˝ to a white rectangle 4½˝ × 3½˝. Press the seam allowance toward the white rectangle.

4. Sew the Step 3 unit to right edge of the Step 2 white rectangle along the *long edge*. Press.

5. Sew this block to the top of a Rose Bud Frame panel image and press.

6. Sew a white rectangle 4½˝ × 5½˝, a yellow rectangle 4½˝ × 5½˝, and a dark blue rectangle 4½˝ × 5½˝ together along the 5½˝ edge. Press.

7. Add the Step 6 unit to the bottom of the Step 5 Rose Bud Frame panel image. Press away from the Rose Bud block. Set aside.

CUTTING COLUMN C

Cut rectangles 4½˝ × 7½˝: 1 green, 1 yellow.

Cut rectangle 4½˝ × 5½˝: 1 white.

Cut rectangles 4½˝ × 3½˝: 1 white, 1 gray.

COLUMN C ASSEMBLY

Sew all rectangles together along the short 4½˝ edge.

1. Sew a yellow rectangle 4½˝ × 7½˝ (piece 1) to a white rectangle 4½˝ × 3½˝ (piece 2)

2. Sew a green rectangle 4½˝ × 7½˝ (piece 3) to a white rectangle 4½˝ × 5½˝ (piece 4).

3. Sew the pairs together and add a gray rectangle 4½˝ × 3½˝ (piece 5) to the end. Press all seam allowances toward piece 1. Set aside.

CUTTING SECTION 4

Cut rectangle 4½˝ × 9½˝: 1 white.

Cut rectangle 4½˝ × 6½˝: 1 white.

Cut rectangle 4½˝ × 5½˝: 1 white.

Cut squares 4½˝ × 4½˝: 1 white, 1 dark blue, 2 orange.

Cut rectangle 4½˝ × 3½˝: 1 medium blue.

SECTION 4 ASSEMBLY

This section consists of a short row of 3 squares and a second section of very short columns. Sew all rectangles together along the short 4½˝ edge.

1. Create a horizontal row of 3 squares by sewing a white square 4½˝ × 4½˝, a dark blue square 4½˝ × 4½˝, and an orange square 4½˝ × 4½˝ together. Press.

2. Sew the Step 1 unit to the top of a Rose Bud Frame panel block. Press the seam allowance toward the squares.

3. Sew an orange square 4½˝ × 4½˝ to a white rectangle 4½˝ × 5½˝. Press the seam allowance toward the white rectangle. Set aside.

4. Sew a white rectangle 4½˝ × 6½˝ to a medium blue rectangle 4½˝ × 3½˝. Press the seam allowance toward the blue.

5. Sew the Step 3 unit to the Step 4 unit and add a white rectangle 4½˝ × 9½˝ to the Step 4 unit. Press.

"""

6. Sew the Step 5 unit to the bottom of the Rose Bud Frame panel block from Step 2. Press the seam allowance toward the rectangles. Set aside.

Central Panel to the Patchwork Assembly

Refer to the quilt assembly diagram (page 115).

1. Sew Section 3, Column C, and Section 4 together. Press the seam allowances toward the column.

2. Sew this unit to the top of the central panel. Press the seam allowance toward the central panel.

3. Sew Column B to the left side of the central panel unit. Press the seam allowance toward the column. Set aside.

CUTTING COLUMN D

Cut rectangle 4½˝ × 7½˝: 1 dark blue.

Cut rectangle 4½˝ × 6½˝: 1 white.

Cut rectangles 4½˝ × 5½˝: 1 gray, 1 green, 1 medium blue, 1 orange.

Cut square 4½˝ × 4½˝: 1 medium blue.

Cut rectangles 4½˝ × 3½˝: 1 white, 1 yellow.

COLUMN D ASSEMBLY

Sew all rectangles together along the short 4½˝ edge.

1. Sew the white rectangle 4½˝ × 6½˝ (piece 1) to a medium blue rectangle 4½˝ × 5½˝ (piece 2).

2. Sew an orange rectangle 4½˝ × 5½˝ (piece 3) to a dark blue rectangle 4½˝ × 7½˝ (piece 4).

3. Sew a green rectangle 4½˝ × 5½˝ (piece 5) to a medium blue square 4½˝ × 4½˝ (piece 6).

4. Sew a white rectangle 4½˝ × 3½˝ (piece 7) to a yellow rectangle 4½˝ × 3½˝ (piece 8).

5. Sew all the pairs together and then sew a gray rectangle 4½˝ × 5½˝ (piece 9) to the end. Press all seam allowances toward piece 1.

CUTTING SECTION 5

Cut rectangles 4½˝ × 7½˝: 2 white, 1 orange, 1 yellow.

Cut rectangle 4½˝ × 6½˝: 1 white.

Cut rectangles 4½˝ × 5½˝: 1 white, 1 green, 1 dark blue, 1 orange.

Cut rectangles 4½˝ × 3½˝: 1 gray, 1 yellow.

SECTION 5 ASSEMBLY

There are 3 short columns that make up this section. Each column will begin with a new piece 1. Sew all rectangles together along the short 4½˝ edge.

1. Sew a yellow rectangle 4½˝ × 3½˝ (piece 1) to an orange rectangle 4½˝ × 5½˝ (piece 2).

2. Sew a dark blue rectangle 4½˝ × 5½˝ (piece 3) to a yellow rectangle 4½˝ × 7½˝ (piece 4).

3. Sew the pairs together and press the seam allowances toward piece 4. Set aside.

4. Sew a white rectangle 4½˝ × 5½˝ (piece 1) to a green rectangle 4½˝ × 5½˝ (piece 2).

5. Sew a white rectangle 4½˝ × 7½˝ (piece 3) to a gray rectangle 3½˝ × 4½˝ (piece 4).

6. Sew the pairs together and press the seam allowances toward piece 4. Set aside.

7. Sew a white rectangle 4½˝ × 7½˝ (piece 1) to an orange rectangle 4½˝ × 7½˝ (piece 2) and add a white rectangle 4½˝ × 6½˝ (piece 3) to the end. Press all seam allowances toward piece 3.

8. Sew the Step 3, Step 6, and Step 7 columns together. Press.

CUTTING SECTION 6

Cut rectangle 4½″ × 6½″: 1 white.

Cut rectangles 4½″ × 5½″: 1 gray, 1 medium blue, 1 orange.

Cut rectangles 4½″ × 3½″: 1 white, 1 green, 1 dark blue, 1 yellow.

SECTION 6 ASSEMBLY

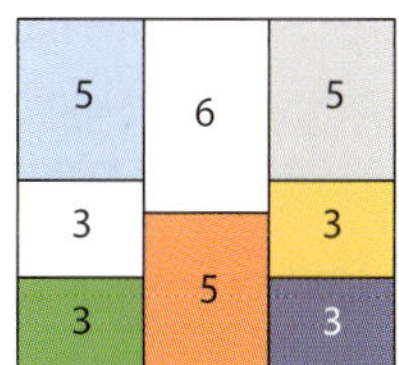

There are 3 short columns that make up this section. Each column will begin with a new piece 1. Sew all rectangles together along the short 4½″ edge.

1. Sew a medium blue rectangle 4½″ × 5½″ (piece 1) to a white rectangle 4½″ × 3½″ (piece 2) and add a green rectangle 4½″ × 3½″ (piece 3) to the end. Press the seam allowances toward piece 3. Set aside.

2. Sew a white rectangle 4½″ × 6½″ (piece 1) to an orange rectangle 4½″ × 5½″ (piece 2). Press the seam allowance toward piece 2.

3. Sew a gray rectangle 4½″ × 5½″ (piece 1) to a yellow rectangle 4½″ × 3½″ (piece 2) and add a dark blue rectangle 4½″ × 3½″ (piece 3) to the end. Press all seam allowances toward piece 3.

4. Sew the 3 columns together and press.

SECTIONS 5–6 ASSEMBLY

Refer to the quilt assembly diagram (page 115).

1. Sew Section 5 to the top of a Rose Bud Frame panel.

2. Sew Section 6 to the bottom of the Rose Bud Frame panel from Step 1. Press both seam allowances away from the Rose Bud block.

COLUMN D AND SECTION 5–6 TO CENTRAL PANEL ASSEMBLY

Refer to the quilt assembly diagram (page 115).

1. Sew Column D to Sections 5–6.

2. Sew this unit to the right side of the central panel unit, being sure that Column D is next to the central panel.

CUTTING SECTION 7

Cut rectangles 4½″ × 8½″: 1 white, 1 yellow.

Cut rectangle 4½″ × 5½″: 1 orange.

Cut rectangles 3½″ × 4½″: 2 white, 1 green, 1 medium blue.

SECTION 7 ASSEMBLY

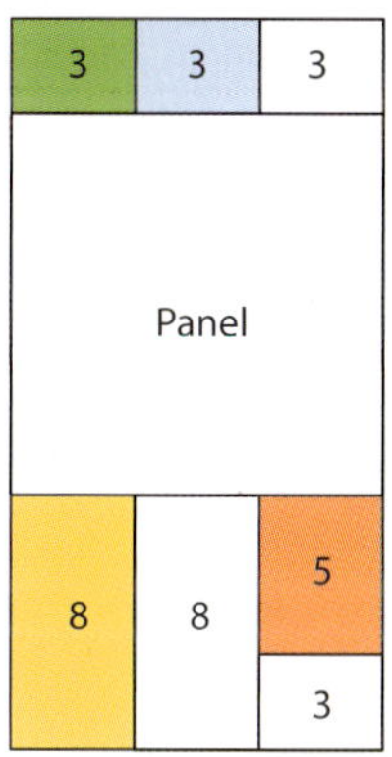

Sew all rectangles together along the short 4½″ edge unless otherwise noted.

1. Create a horizontal row by sewing a green rectangle 4½″ × 3½″ (piece 1), a medium blue rectangle 4½″ × 3½″ (piece 2), and a white rectangle 4½″ × 3½″ (piece 3) together along the short edges. Press the seam allowances toward piece 3.

2. Sew this row of rectangles to the top of a Rose Bud Frame panel block. Press the seam allowance toward the rectangles.

3. Sew a yellow rectangle 4½″ × 8½″ to a white rectangle 4½″ × 8½″ along the long edges. Press.

4. Sew an orange 4½″ × 5½″ rectangle to a white 4½″ × 3½″ rectangle. Press.

5. Sew the Step 3 unit to the Step 4 unit. Press.

6. Sew this unit to the bottom of the Rose Bud Frame panel block. Press the seam allowance toward the rectangles.

CUTTING SECTION 8

Cut rectangle 4½″ × 8½″: 1 white.

Cut rectangles 4½″ × 7½″: 2 white, 2 green, 1 yellow.

Cut rectangles 4½″ × 6½″: 1 white, 1 orange.

Cut rectangles 4½″ × 5½″: 3 white, 1 dark blue, 2 medium blue.

Cut square 4½″ × 4½″: 1 yellow.

Cut rectangle 4½″ × 3½″: 1 gray.

SECTION 8 ASSEMBLY

There are 4 short columns that make up this section. Each column will begin with a new piece 1. Sew all rectangles together along the short 4½˝ edge.

1. Sew a yellow square 4½˝ × 4½˝ (piece 1) to a white rectangle 4½˝ × 5½˝ (piece 2).

2. Sew a green rectangle 4½˝ × 7½˝ (piece 3) to a white rectangle 4½˝ × 7½˝ (piece 4).

3. Sew the pairs together and press all seam allowances toward piece 1. Set aside.

4. Sew an orange rectangle 4½˝ × 6½˝ (piece 1) to a dark blue rectangle 4½˝ × 5½˝ (piece 2).

5. Sew a white rectangle 4½˝ × 7½˝ (piece 3) to a medium blue rectangle 4½˝ × 5½˝ (piece 4).

6. Sew the pairs together and press all seam allowances toward piece 4. Set aside.

7. Sew a green rectangle 4½˝ × 7½˝ (piece 1) to a white rectangle 4½˝ × 5½˝ (piece 2).

8. Sew a gray rectangle 4½˝ × 3½˝ (piece 3) to a white rectangle 4½˝ × 8½˝ (piece 4).

9. Sew the pairs together and press all seam allowances toward piece 1. Set aside.

10. Sew a white rectangle 4½˝ × 5½˝ (piece 1) to a medium blue rectangle 4½˝ × 5½˝ (piece 2).

11. Sew a yellow rectangle 4½˝ × 7½˝ (piece 3) to a white rectangle 4½˝ × 6½˝ (piece 4).

12. Sew the pairs together and press all seam allowances toward piece 4.

13. Sew the 4 columns together and press.

CUTTING SECTION 9

Cut rectangle 4½˝ × 7½˝: 1 dark blue.

Cut squares 4½˝ × 4½˝: 1 white, 1 green, 1 medium blue, 2 orange.

Cut rectangles 4½˝ × 3½˝: 1 dark blue, 1 yellow.

SECTION 9 ASSEMBLY

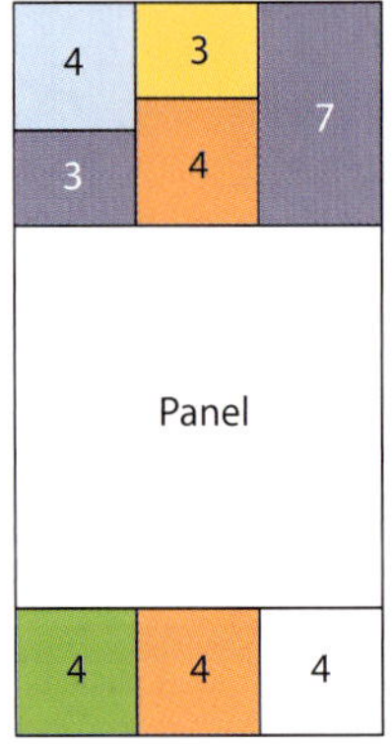

Sew all rectangles together along the short 4½˝ edge.

1. Sew a medium blue square 4½˝ × 4½˝ to a dark blue rectangle 4½˝ × 3½˝. Press and set aside.

2. Sew a yellow rectangle 4½˝ × 3½˝ to an orange square 4½˝ × 4½˝. Press.

3. Sew the Step 1 and Step 2 units together and add a dark blue rectangle 4½˝ × 7½˝ to the Step 2 unit. Press.

4. Sew this unit to the top of a Rose Bud Frame panel image. Press the seam allowance toward the rectangles.

5. Sew a row with a green square 4½˝ × 4½˝, an orange square 4½˝ × 4½˝, and a white square 4½˝ × 4½˝. Press.

6. Sew this unit to the bottom of the Rose Bud Frame panel image. Press the seam allowance toward the rectangles. Set aside.

CUTTING SECTION 10

Cut rectangles 4½˝ × 3½˝: 2 gray, 1 yellow.

Cut rectangles 4½˝ × 5½˝: 1 white, 1 green, 1 orange.

Cut rectangles 4½˝ × 7½˝: 1 white, 1 medium blue.

Cut squares 4½˝ × 4½˝: 1 white, 1 dark blue.

SECTION 10 ASSEMBLY

There are 2 short columns that make up this section. Each column will begin with a new piece 1. Sew all rectangles together along the short 4½˝ edge.

1. Sew a white rectangle 4½˝ × 7½˝ (piece 1) to a yellow rectangle 4½˝ × 3½˝ (piece 2).

2. Sew a green rectangle 4½˝ × 5½˝ (piece 3) to a white rectangle 4½˝ × 5½˝ (piece 4).

3. Sew the pairs together and add a gray rectangle 4½˝ × 3½˝ (piece 5) to the end. Press all seam allowances toward piece 5.

4. Sew a gray rectangle 4½˝ × 43½˝ (piece 1) to a white square 4½˝ × 4½˝ (piece 2).

5. Sew an orange rectangle 4½˝ × 5½˝ (piece 3) to a medium blue rectangle 4½˝ × 7½˝ (piece 4).

6. Sew the pairs together and add a dark blue square 4½˝ × 4½˝ (piece 5) to the end. Press all seam allowances toward piece 1.

7. Sew the columns together and press.

Sections 7–10 Assembly

Refer to the quilt assembly diagram (below).

1. Sew Sections 7–10 together along the long edges. Press.

2. Sew the combined unit to the bottom of the central panel unit. Press.

ADDING COLUMNS A AND E

1. Sew Column A to the left side of Sections 1–2 and then sew this unit to the body of the quilt. Press.

2. Sew Column E to the right side of the body of the quilt. Press. *fig. A*

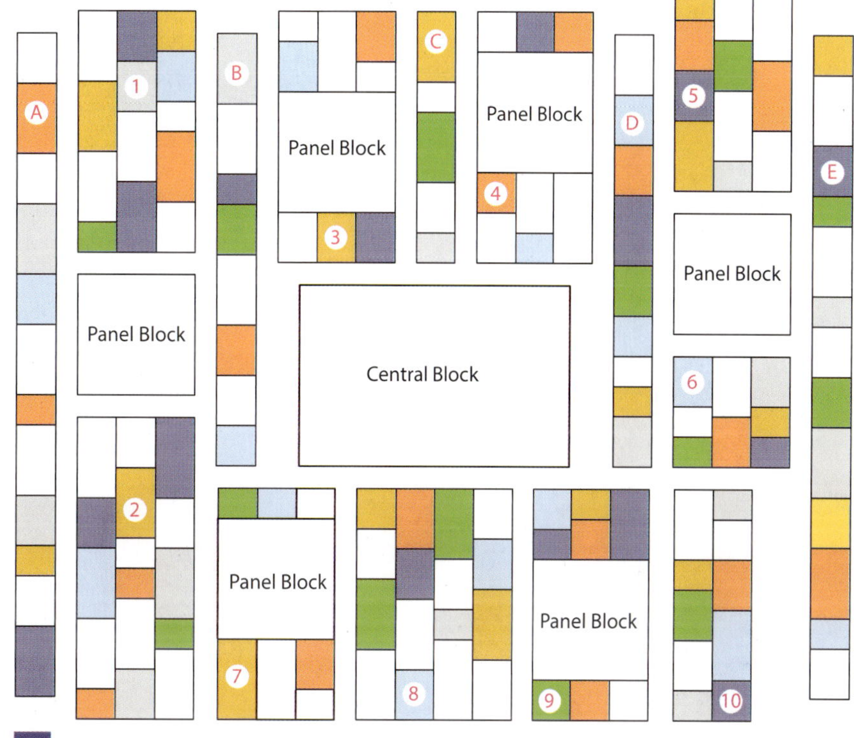

A Quilt assembly

Borders

CUTTING

Cut 36 white squares 3½˝ × 3½˝.

Cut 7 or 8 squares 3½˝ × 3½˝ each from green, dark blue, medium blue, yellow, and orange for a total of 36.

SIDE BORDERS ASSEMBLY

1. Sew 2 strips 2½˝ × WOF end to end and trim to 2½˝ × 66½˝. Make 2.

2. Sew a border to each side of the quilt body and press the seam allowance to the border.

HSTS FOR TOP AND BOTTOM BORDERS

Pair a colored square 3½˝ × 3½˝ with a white square 3½˝ × 3½˝ to make 2 HSTs. Make 72 HSTs. Press and trim to 2½˝ × 2½˝.

TOP AND BOTTOM BORDER ASSEMBLY

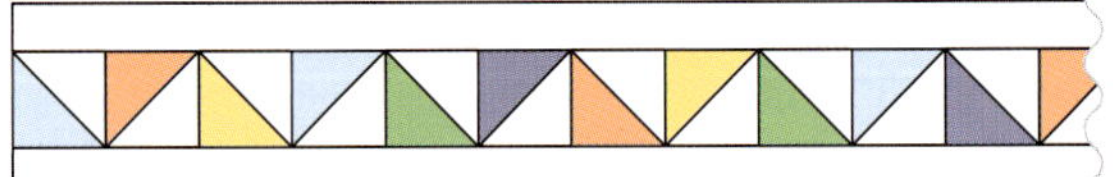

1. Sew 2 strips 1½˝ × WOF end to end and trim to 1½˝ × 72½˝. Make 4.

2. Alternating the direction of the HSTs, piece together 36 HSTs to create a border for the top and bottom.

3. Sew a 1½˝ × 72½˝ white border to each side of both HST borders.

4. Sew a border unit to the top and bottom of the quilt.

FINISHING

1. Quilt, bind, and add a hanging sleeve, if desired.

2. Enjoy!

Make It Your Own!

Chirping Christmas by Terry Helmer

Terry's panel, *Believe*, from Henry Glass

Terry chose this beautiful panel *Believe* from Henry Glass and a wintry mix of coordinates to complete her version of this quilt. Because her panel had only 4 coordinating images, she substituted the County Fair quilt block in 2 of the spaces from the original pattern to honor her many years of service to her county fair in Colorado. For other suitable blocks to substitute, see Alternate Blocks for 8˝ × 8˝ Finished Size Panel Images (page 16).

Large Tote Bag

FINISHED BAG:
20½″ WIDE × 21″ TALL × 5″ DEEP

Design Suggestions

Have you ever wondered what to do with those 2-image panels? The artwork is great, so perhaps turning them into something you can show off at your next get-together would be a fun way to incorporate them into a useful project!

I used panels from Riley Blake for both of these projects. *Perennial* and *Sewing Seeds III Pillow Sham Panel* panels feature 2 large images. They were perfect for my jumbo bags!

Materials

*Yardages are based on
41˝-wide fabric.*

Panel: 1–2 panel images
adjustable to 21˝ × 21˝. I
used *Perennial* and *Sewing
Seeds III Pillow Sham Panel*
by Riley Blake.

Bag fabric: ⅝ yard (if you
only have 1 panel to use)

**Medium-weight fusible
stabilizer:** ¼ yard (optional
1⅛ yards at 58˝ WOF; see
below)

**Red for lining, handles,
sides, and bottom of bag:**
2¼ yards

Cutting

Panel

Trim and square 1 or
2 panel images to 21˝ × 21˝.

Bag Fabric

Cut 1 square 21˝ × 21˝ (if
you're using only 1 panel).

Red

Cut 2 strips 3½˝ × 21˝.

Cut 2 strips 3½˝ × 47˝.

Cut 2 strips 5˝ × 22˝.

Cut 2 lining pieces
25˝ × 26½˝.

Stabilizer

Cut 1 rectangle 5˝ × 20˝.

CONSTRUCTION

Construct by using a ½˝ seam allowance.

Press all seam allowances open unless otherwise noted.

If you decide to use the optional stabilizer, fuse it to all cut pieces except the
blue handles 5˝ × 22˝.

1. Sew a red strip 3½˝ × 21˝ to the bottom of each panel image. Press the
seam allowance toward the red strip.

2. Sew the front and back of the bag,
right sides together, along the
bottom red strips 3½˝ × 21˝. Press
the seam allowances open. *fig. A*

3. Sew a red strip 3½˝ × 47˝ to
each side of the central panel
section. Press the seam allowance
toward the strips. *fig. B*

4. Center the stabilizer 5˝ × 21˝ on
the bottom red strips and fuse.

5. Fold the bag, right sides
together, so the panel images are facing each other and sew the side seams.
Backstitch at the start and finish of the seam. Press.

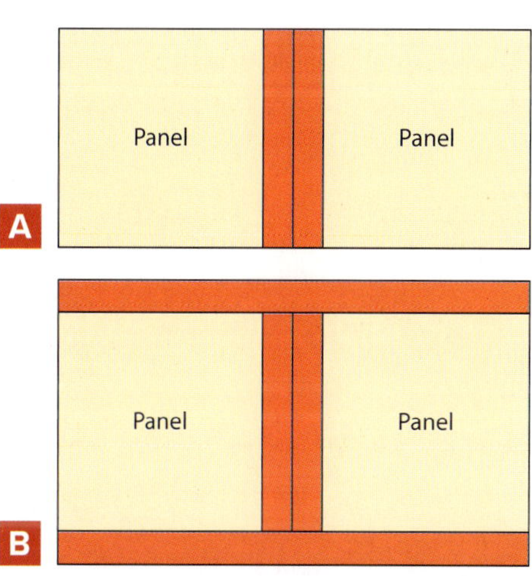

6. Create boxed corners by pulling the front and back of the bag away from each other to form a triangle at the bottom. Match the bottom seam with the side seam and pin.

7. Measure 2½″ from the tip of the triangle and draw a line along the base of the triangle. Stitch on the line, being sure to backstitch at both ends. You may wish to catch the edge of the stabilizer in your stitching.

8. Cut away the triangle ½″ from the stitching. *fig. C*

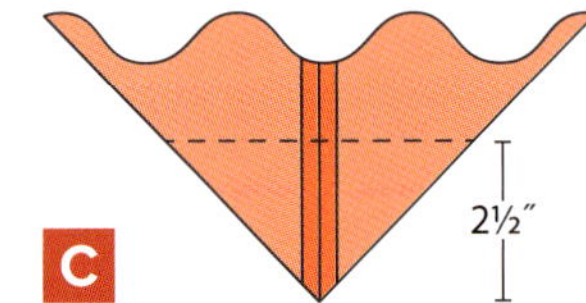

9. Turn the bag right side out and push the corners into shape by using a point turner.

10. Fold the top of the bag 1″ to the inside and press.

11. Sew the 2 lining pieces, right sides together, down a 25″ side, across the 26½″ bottom, and back up the other side, backstitching at the start and finish of the seams. Press.

12. Create boxed corners by pulling the front and back of the lining away from each other to form a triangle at the bottom. Match the side and bottom seams and pin.

13. Measure 2½″ from the tip of the triangle and draw a line along the base of the triangle. Stitch on the line, being sure to backstitch at both ends.

14. Cut away the triangle ½″ from the stitching.

15. Fold the red strips 5″ × 22″ in half lengthwise, wrong sides together, and press.

16. Open the strip and fold each half lengthwise into the center crease, wrong sides together. Press. *fig. D*

17. Fold again on the center crease and press. Stitch ⅛″ from each folded edge.

18. Mark the center of each side of the lining. Pin one end of each handle 5″ away from the center line, matching the raw edge of the handle to the raw edge of the hem. Stitch on the inside of the lining by sewing a scant 1″ square with an X through it to secure the handles to the lining. Repeat for the other end of the handle.

19. Repeat for the other handle on the other side of the lining.

20. Fold the top edge of the lining 1″ to the inside and press.

21. Place the lining inside the outer fabric, matching the side seams and being sure that the upper edges are still folded down.

22. Match the top edges and the side seams and pin all the way around the bag. Topstitch ¼″ from the top of the bag. Topstitch again ⅛″ from the edge of the bag.

23. Push the lining boxed corners into the boxed corners of the outer-bag corners.

24. Enjoy!

TEMPLATES

Scan the QR code or visit the website below to access
the templates for this book.

tinyurl.com/11635-patterns-download

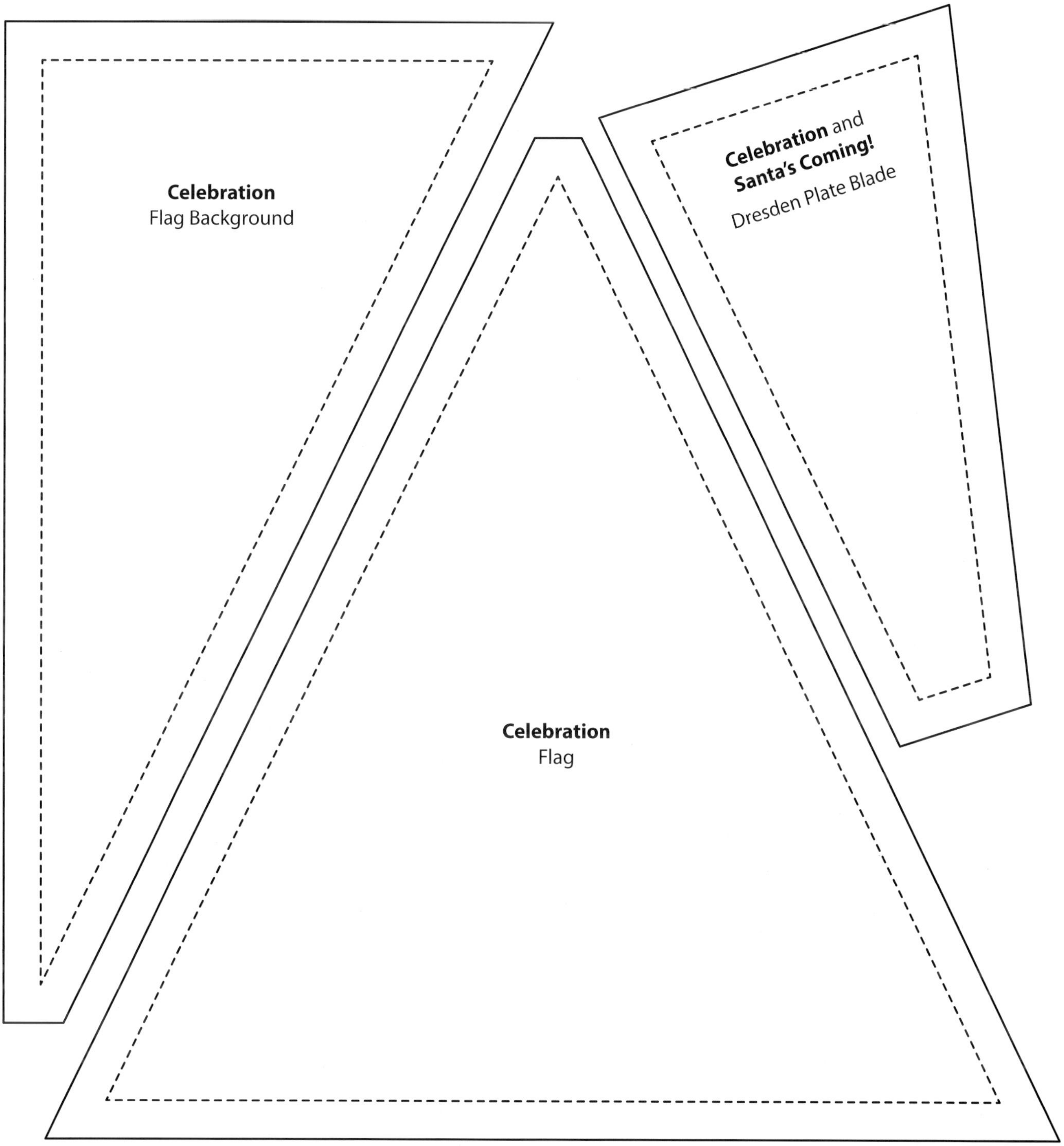

Celebration
Flag Background

Celebration and
Santa's Coming!
Dresden Plate Blade

Celebration
Flag

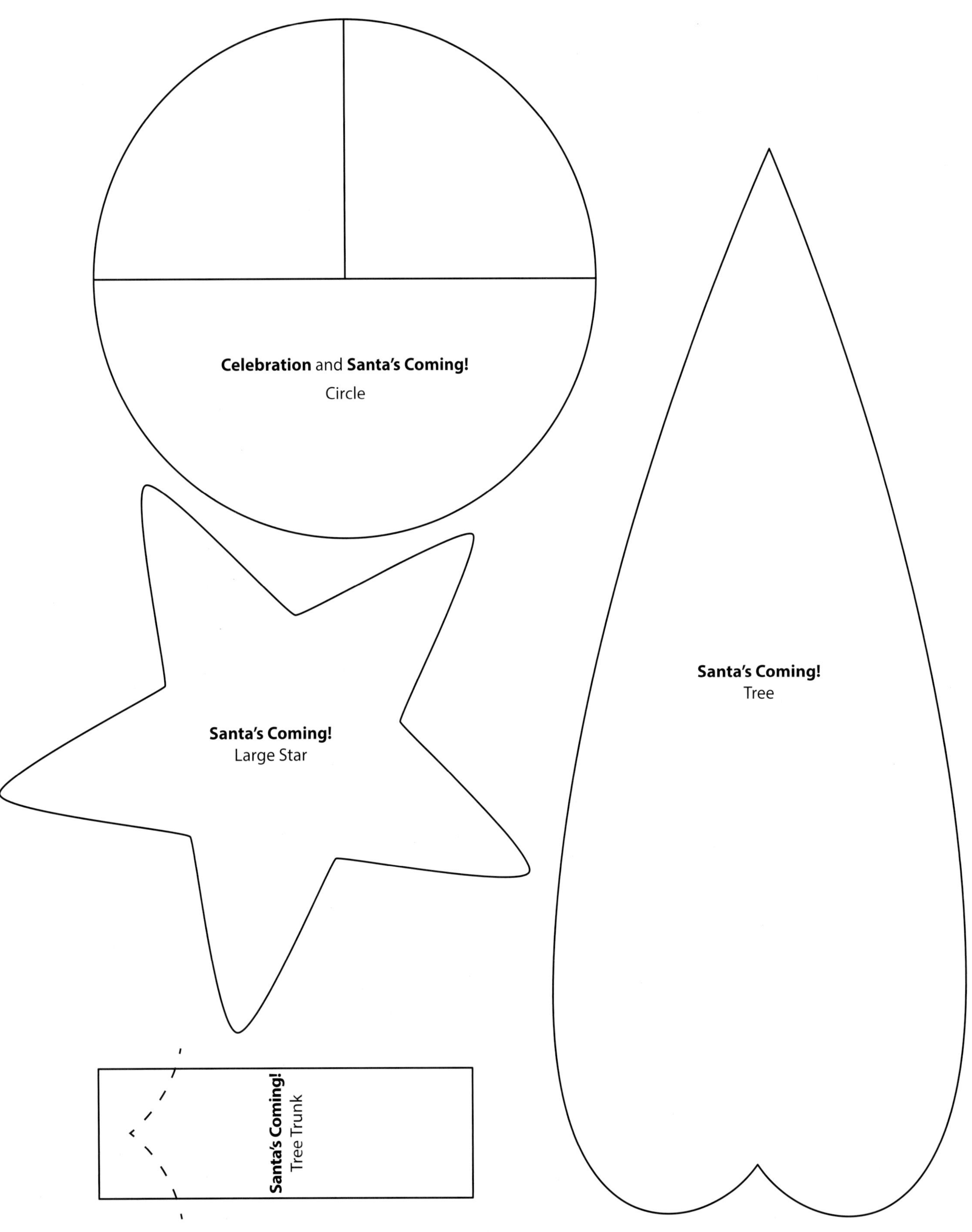

Celebration and Santa's Coming!
Circle
Santa's Coming!
Large Star
Santa's Coming!
Tree Trunk
Santa's Coming!
Tree

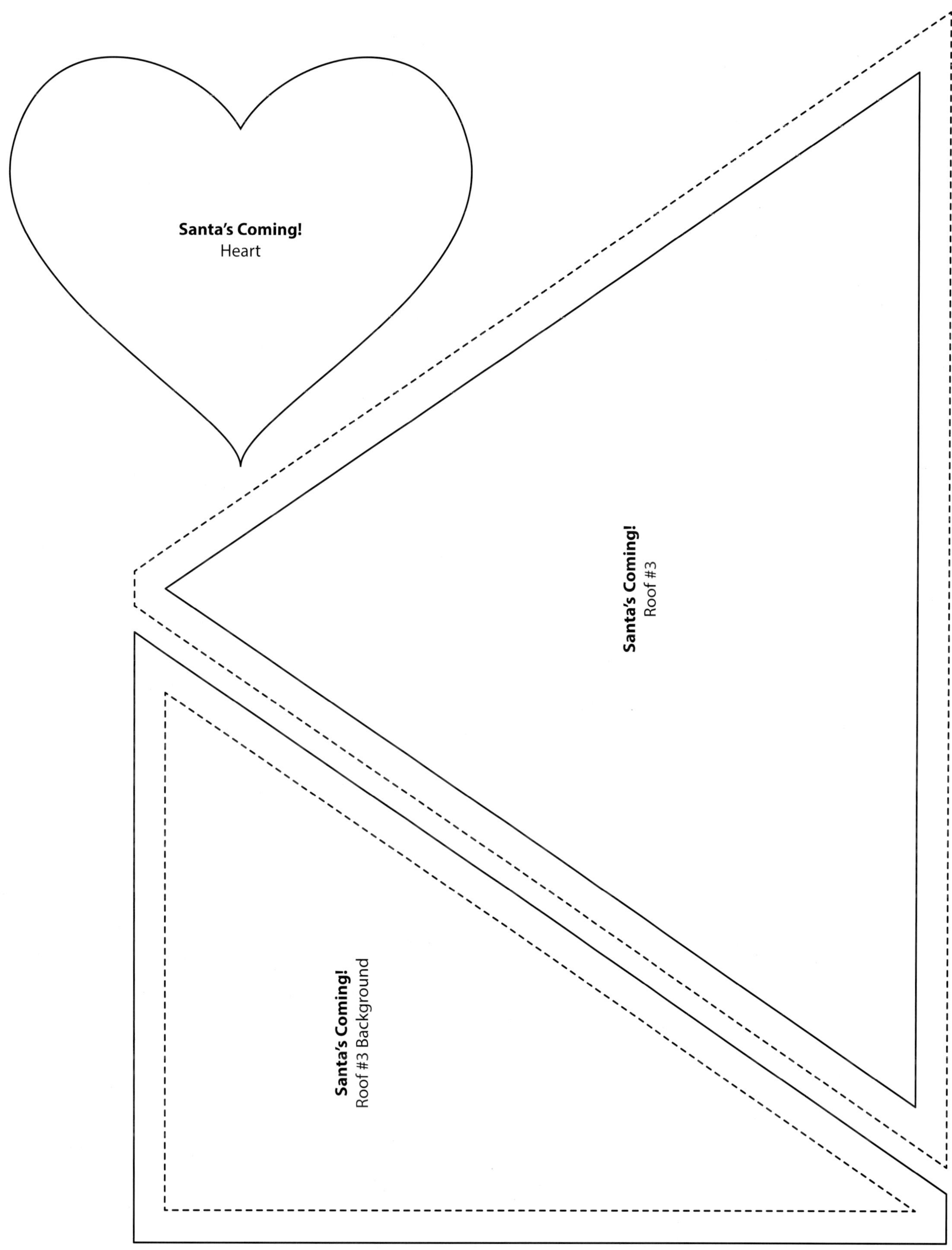

Santa's Coming!
Heart

Santa's Coming!
Roof #3

Santa's Coming!
Roof #3 Background

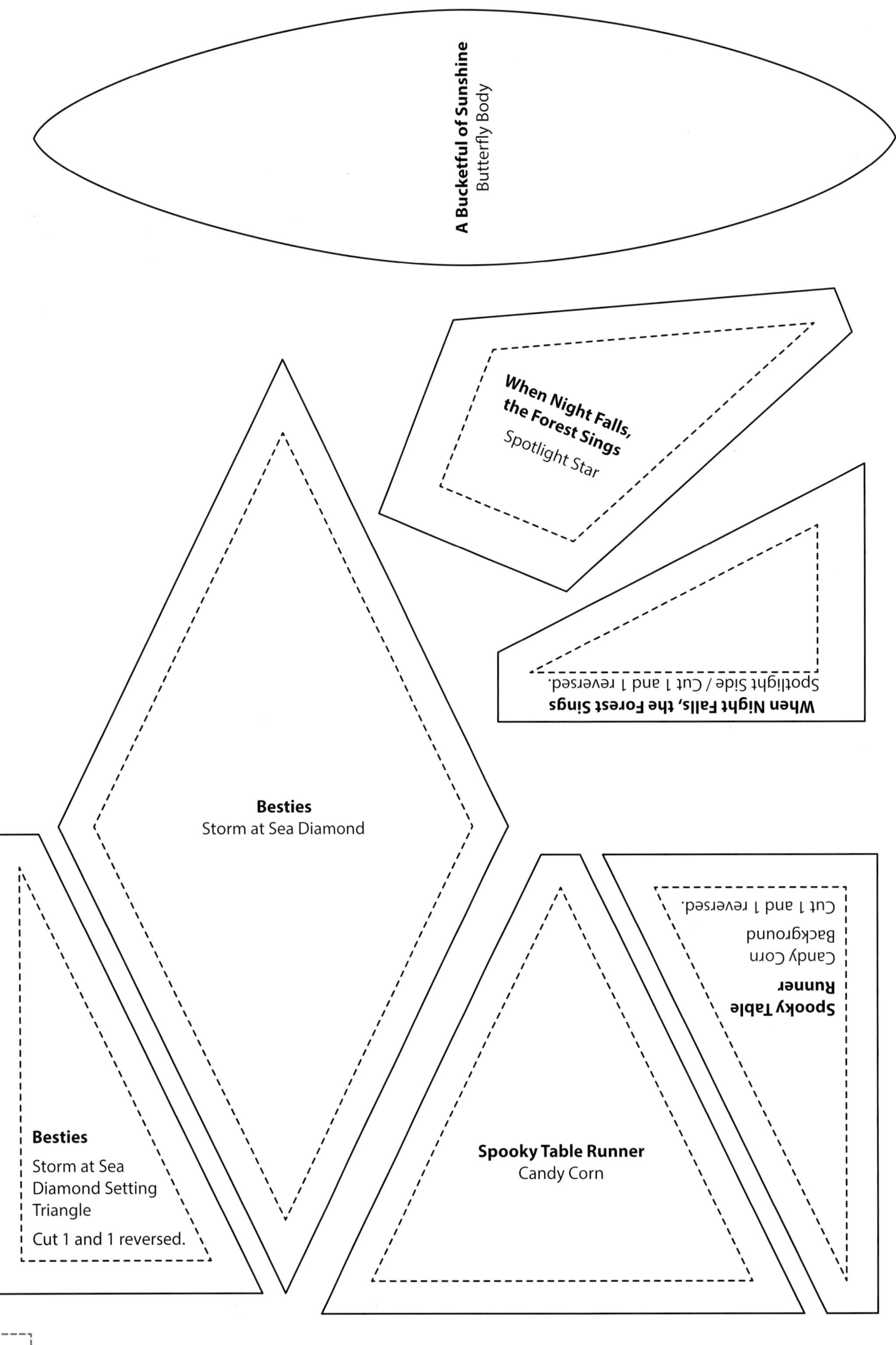

A Bucketful of Sunshine
Butterfly Body
When Night Falls, the Forest Sings
Spotlight Star
When Night Falls, the Forest Sings
Spotlight Side / Cut 1 and 1 reversed.
Besties
Storm at Sea Diamond
Besties
Storm at Sea Diamond Setting Triangle
Cut 1 and 1 reversed.
Spooky Table Runner
Candy Corn
Spooky Table Runner
Candy Corn Background
Cut 1 and 1 reversed.

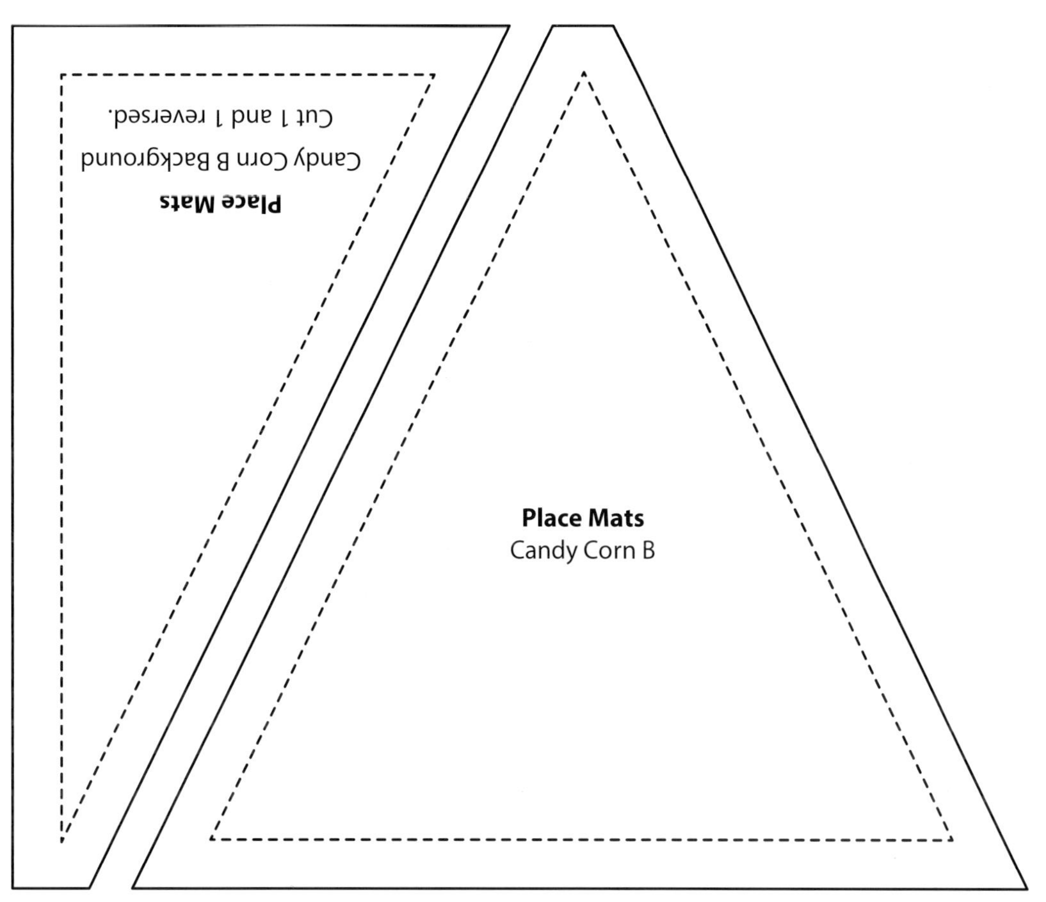

Place Mats
Candy Corn B Background
Cut 1 and 1 reversed.
Place Mats
Candy Corn B

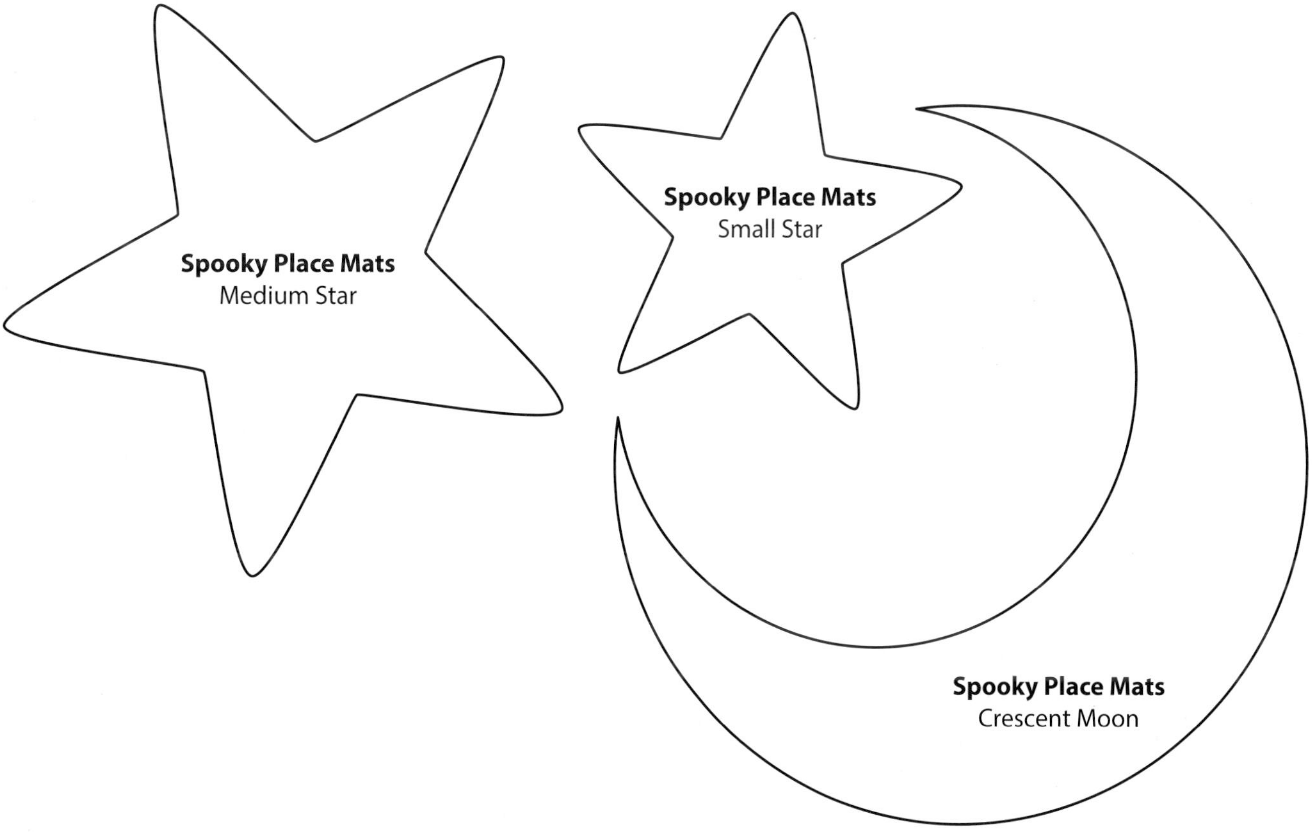

Spooky Place Mats
Medium Star
Spooky Place Mats
Small Star
Spooky Place Mats
Crescent Moon

Resources

The New Ladies Art Company Quick & Easy Block Tool, by Connie Chunn (C&T Publishing)

The New Quick & Easy Block Tool, edited by Liz Aneloski, Kandy Petersen, and Debbie Rodgers (C&T Publishing)

Gridded Paper Pad: 4 × 4 Grid (Bienfang)

Easy Dresden Tool by Darlene Zimmerman (EZ Quilting)

Tri-Recs Tool

ABOUT THE CONTRIBUTORS

This amazing team of quilters was such a gift in helping this book come to be. Each of them enthusiastically agreed to try out one of these patterns with a different panel, sometimes adding their own flair, substituting a block or appliqué motif or changing things up in unexpected but oh-so-wonderful ways! I hope their work inspires you to do the same!

Marie Clanton

I have been a sewist all my adult life, then I started taking classes and piecing various quilt tops off and on in 2004. I finally got serious in 2010 and have been addicted ever since. I tried different patterns and styles until I made my first panel quilt in 2015, and that was it for me! I find working with panels challenging and deeply rewarding.

Terry Helmer

In the late 1990s, in Florida, I made one quilt and a quilted jacket. In 2000, illness prevented me from working, and normal life was difficult for the next fifteen years. However, the urge to quilt was still there. I was blessed with a miracle in 2016 that gave me my life back, and I started quilting again, prolifically this time, completing many projects. I have wonderful friends in the quilting community, and I love having opportunities to improve my skills.

Adam Holladay

I started my quilt journey while sitting in the "man's chair" in a quilt store in 2004 as my wife was shopping for fabric. While looking at a Sunbonnet Sue pattern, I had an idea to replace those blocks with different birds. One full-size Redwork embroidered bird quilt later, I was hooked. My motto: "Go big or go home"; thus king size is my preference. Cyndi was more than eager to assist me on this journey with her many classes!

Tonya Hubbard

Tonya has been quilting for many years and has completed quilts ranging from simple scrappy quilts to complex paper-pieced designs. One of her greatest joys is meeting new quilters who have a shared interest in quilting, which often sparks conversations that blossom into lasting friendships. She believes that the true beauty of quilting lies not just in the quilts themselves but in the connections made along the way. With every stop at a quilt shop, quilt class, or quilt retreat, Tonya discovers new stories, experiences, and kindred spirits in the quilting community.

Heikei Kovacich

Heikei Kovacich made her first quilt more than 30 years ago. When life got busy with family and work, quilting went by the wayside. In 2020, she attended a home and garden show, and there was a booth for a sewing/quilting store. She signed up for a beginner's quilting class and was lucky enough to meet Cyndi McChesney and have her as the instructor for this class. It ignited an old flame, and she was off and running. *Liam's Quilt* is the tenth quilt she has made since then. Liam is her grandson, and he loves cats, dogs, and bright colors. What an amazing gift this is going to be! Thanks to Cyndi for including her in this project, it's quite a blessing!

Margaret Matchett

There were always quilts on the beds in my childhood home in Texas … That's probably where I caught the quilting bug. I made my first twin-size quilt top after my freshman year away at college. It was kind of a clumsy Pinwheel, but it was pretty and colorful. Piecing quilts has been part of my life since then, albeit in the background while working as a programmer and as a teacher, but now I am retired and have more time and MUCH more fabric.

Jacki Montplaisar

I started my quilt journey before rotary cutters, tracing cardboard templates onto fabric and cutting shapes with scissors! I have stitch pieced, appliquéd, paper pieced, and English paper pieced quilts of all sizes and shapes. Cyndi has been a mentor and inspiration in my quilting journey!

Kathryn Oliphant

I live in Colorado Springs, Colorado, with my husband and an energetic Corgi named Jily. I have been sewing forever but started quilting about ten years ago. I believe every bed should have three or four quilts on it to celebrate the seasons— or even just for fun!

Laura Tanner

After retiring in 2012, I took Cyndi's beginners quilting class. She made it so much fun that I haven't stopped since.

Susan Wiley

Susan was introduced to quilting several years ago by attending a class with her best friend, who was already hooked. She quickly fell in love with the beautiful choices of fabrics and the many challenging quilt possibilities. With an artist's background, she enjoys combining traditional quilt patterns with her own design twists. Her advice for beginning quilters: "Once you get started, the possibilities are endless. Just get into your workspace and play!"

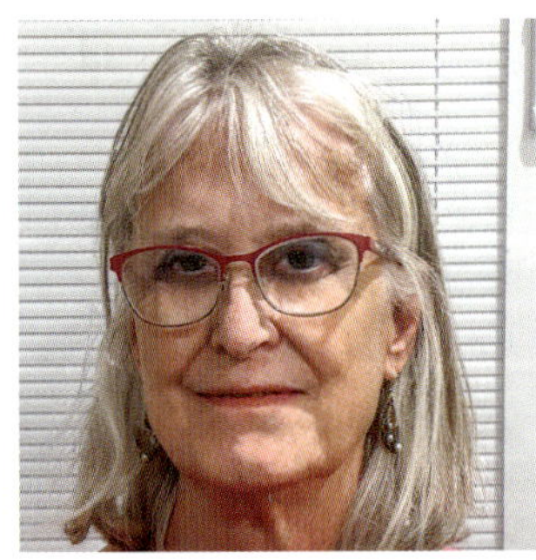

About the Author

Cyndi is a passionate cyclist, hiker, and explorer and gets outdoors regularly with her dog, Strider. She enjoys time in nature every day and loves to discover new places to enjoy a quiet cup of tea and the local arts and crafts communities.

One of Cyndi's greatest joys is to challenge students to embrace techniques that will enhance their ability to create unusual and unique designs. In her workshops, with detailed guidance, she encourages students to step out of their comfort zone and express themselves with confidence. She challenges quilters to explore working with panels, as they offer a surprising window into the world of designing one's own unique projects and quilts.

As a much-sought-after instructor, Cyndi enjoys teaching throughout the United States and Canada and is known for her humorous and detailed teaching expertise. She presents her educational and entertaining trunk show, Panel Palooza; teaches in person and online; and hosts several on-demand classes through C&T's Creative Spark platform.

Correspondence may be sent directly to Cyndi via email at **cyndimcchesney@gmail.com**

Look for upcoming classes from Cyndi on C&T's teaching platform, Creative Spark!

Website: **cedarridgequilting.com**